FLORIDA STATE
UNIVERSITY LIBRARIES

JUL 27 2000

TALLAHASSEE, FLORIDA

The Working-Class Movement in America

The Working-Class Movement in America
by Eleanor Marx and Edward Aveling

Edited with an Introduction by
Paul Le Blanc

with Essays by
Lisa Frank and Kim Moody

Humanity Books

an imprint of Prometheus Books
59 John Glenn Drive, Amherst, New York 14228-2197

Published 2000 by Humanity Books, an imprint of Prometheus Books

The Working-Class Movement in America. Copyright © 2000 Paul Le Blanc. All rights reserved. No part of this publication may be reproduced, stored in a retrieval system, or transmitted in any form or by any means, digital, electronic, mechanical, photocopying, recording, or otherwise, or conveyed via the Internet or a website without prior written permission of the publisher, except in the case of brief quotations embodied in critical articles and reviews.

Inquiries should be addressed to
Humanity Books
59 John Glenn Drive
Amherst, New York 14228–2197
VOICE: 716–691–0133, ext. 207
FAX: 716–564–2711

04 03 02 01 00   5 4 3 2 1

Library of Congress Cataloging-in-Publication Data

Aveling, Eleanor Marx, 1855–1898
   The working class movement in America / [Eleanor Marx and Edward Aveling ; edited with an introd. by Paul LeBlanc ; with essays by Lisa Frank and Kim Moody].
      p. cm. — (Revolutionary series)
   Rev. ed. of: The working class movement in America / Edward Aveling and Eleanor Marx, 2d ed. 1891.
   Includes bibliographical references and index.
   ISBN 1-57392-626-4
   1. Working class—United States—History. 2. Labor movement—United States—History. 3. Labor leaders—United States—History. I. Aveling, Edward Bibbins, 1851–1898. Working class movement in America. II. LeBlanc, Paul, 1957– III. Title. IV. Series.

HD8066 .A95 2000
331.1'0973'09034—dc21   99-089708
                                                                        CIP

Printed in the United States of America on acid-free paper

Contents

Introduction: Making Sense of
The Working-Class Movement in America
    Paul Le Blanc   7

Essay: On the Uses of Eleanor Marx
    Lisa Frank   37

The Working-Class Movement in America
Edward Aveling and Eleanor Marx-Aveling

1. Introduction   69

2. General Impressions   75

3. The General Condition of American Workers   81

4. The Conduct of Employers   91

5. Wages, Work, Method of Living   103

6. Woman and Child Labor — 115

7. Organizations—Trade Unions and the Grange — 133

8. Knights of Labor—Central Labor Unions—Socialistic Labor Party—United Labor Party — 141

9. The Cowboys — 153

10. Anarchists — 159

11. Some Working-Class Leaders — 171

12. Appendix — 189

Note to Chapters 8 and 10 — 203

Essay: After the Tour
 Kim Moody — 209

Index — 223

Introduction
Making Sense of *The Working-Class Movement in America*
by Paul Le Blanc

This volume includes three items: first, a penetrating essay by cultural historian Lisa Frank on Eleanor Marx, the daughter of Karl Marx (founder of the scientific-socialist orientation that was later labeled "Marxism"); next, and most important, an account of the American working class by Eleanor Marx and Edward Aveling; and third, a stimulating reflection by labor analyst and journalist Kim Moody on the relevance of this century-old report for today's labor movement. My own introductory remarks will touch on the significance of the Marx-Aveling book for the discipline of labor history.

The account published by Eleanor Marx and Edward Aveling is a remarkable document, offering a literary "snapshot" of the U.S. working class near the end of the nineteenth century. It is instructive to compare the realities that impressed them with the realities of our own time. In each period, we see tremendous ferment within a working class, which is responding to profound transformations in an inherently dynamic capitalist society.

In the 1880s, Marx and Aveling discovered vibrant critical

thinking and a growing radicalism (in the sense of seeking to "go to the root" of the problems) among various layers of the working class. As is the case today, few American workers of that time knew anything about Marxian socialist doctrines that (a) traced class struggle between workers and capitalists to the exploitative essence of the capitalist economic system and that (b) envisioned an outcome in which the economy would be socially owned and democratically controlled to guarantee the free development of all people, which is how Karl Marx envisioned socialism.

Back then, such doctrines were comparatively fresh and crisp, not yet frozen into grotesque shapes by the Ice Age of Stalinist dictatorship, and not yet inundated by capitalism's Niagara of anti-Marxist propaganda on the one hand and the gushing fountains of academic Marxism and "post-Marxism" on the other. In 1886 and 1887, many Americans had a half-formed set of perceptions, inclinations, hopes, and values which added up, in the opinion of Eleanor Marx and her companion, to a sort of "unconscious socialism." Would the two have drawn similar conclusions if a time machine had brought them back to the United States in the following century? Seeming to echo the Marx-Aveling observation, but giving it a perverse twist in the Depression years of the early 1930s, an idiosyncratic leftist named Leon Samson argued that a popular ideology of "Americanism"—which embraced radical-democratic and egalitarian values, similar to those underlying Marxism—had taken the place of, and in some ways blocked the development of, a socialist-oriented working-class consciousness. In the economic affluence and repressive political conformism of the early 1950s, ex-Marxist historians, political scientists, and sociologists (Daniel Boorstin, Louis Hartz, Seymour Martin Lipset, Daniel Bell, and others) developed this notion in various ways, in some cases concluding that this was all for the best—that American capitalism blending with democratic traditions had more or less fulfilled the hopes and needs that were supposed to have propelled the masses toward socialism. In the same period, left-wing social critic C. L. R. James drew far more revolutionary conclusions from his studies of popular consciousness within American civilization, and James's notion of revolutionary elements in the consciousness of the U.S. working class—similar to the "unconscious socialism" seen by Marx-Aveling—make even more sense, perhaps, one century after the publication of *The Working-Class Movement in America*, as difficult economic shifts once again seem to pit capitalist development against democratic and egalitarian elements deeply rooted in our popular culture.[1]

In the United States of the 1880s, the two visitors discovered scores of working-class and prolabor newspapers, reflecting vital working-class and labor-radical subcultures. While one could argue that there are insurgent working-class, oppositional, and dissident elements in the popular culture of today, the power of the corporations dominating the multifaceted "entertainment industry," as well as the news and opinion-making industries, seem to have crowded out much of the widespread self-expression and independent cultural activity so prevalent in the working class a hundred years ago. Nonetheless, the ferment of our own time seems, in the eyes of some radical social critics, to create dramatic possibilities for change. Without question, Marx and Aveling had a similar view of the United States as the 1880s were fading into the 1890s: we see them anticipating a formidable proletarian challenge to the bourgeois status quo that presumably would soon be generated by the still-mushrooming Knights of Labor, the still-radical American Federation of Labor, the militant struggles for an eight-hour workday, the widespread labor party efforts, and the growing clusters of organized socialists.

WHAT MARX AND AVELING MISSED

Of course, what Marx and Aveling wrote about the United States could not be more than the impressions gained from a brief tour, and it is important to recognize the profound changes taking place in the U.S. working class which neither Marx nor Aveling was able to see clearly. As Karl Marx and Frederick Engels had commented in the *Communist Manifesto* of 1848, capitalism is a unique system which involves the "constant revolutionizing of production, uninterrupted disturbance of all social conditions, everlasting uncertainty and agitation," in which—over and over again—it seems that "all that is solid melts into air." The United States, which by 1890 would be the world's foremost manufacturing nation, was undergoing remarkable changes, fundamentally altering the realities which these insightful optimists sought to describe. "The structural changes that transformed United States society in the half century from 1865 to 1920," labor historian Melvyn Dubofsky has commented, "continuously reshaped the composition of the working class," to the extent that in retrospect it gives the impression of being "in a state of permanent flux rather than a class in process of formation." The Marx-Aveling account is like a single frame, or at most a brief scene, from a motion-picture. It provides an opportunity to study some fascinating and salient details (and suggestive possibilities), but some of the dynamics and trajectories inherent in this "scene" necessarily eluded them.[2]

Worth analyzing, first of all, is the failure of the initial labor party stirrings to yield any durable alternative to the procapitalist Republican and Democratic parties. In 1887 Frederick Engels—sharing his friends' hopes—hailed the first political steps through which "the laboring masses should feel their community of grievances and of interests, their solidarity as a class in opposition to all other classes," although he was concerned that the embryonic labor party "find the common remedy for these common grievances" and eventually advance this remedy (socialism) in its party platform. Such hopes were bitterly disappointed: not only did the mass political insurgency fail to embrace socialism, but it soon collapsed and was largely reabsorbed by the Democratic and Republican parties. In an 1893 letter, Engels sought to explain why "American conditions involve very great and peculiar difficulties for a steady development of a workers' party." The three factors he identified—imperfectly grasped in the Marx-Aveling account—have become ingredients in the analyses of innumerable historians seeking to explain the absence of a labor party and socialist movement in the United States:

> First, the Constitution, based as in England upon party government, which makes it appear as though every vote were *lost* that is cast for a candidate not put up by one of the two governing parties. And the American, like the Englishman, wants to exert an influence on his state; he does not want to throw his vote away.
>
> Then, and more especially, immigration, which divides the workers into two groups: the native-born and the foreigners, and the latter in turn into (1) the Irish, (2) the Germans, (3) the many small groups—Czechs, Poles, Italians, Scandinavians, etc.—who understand only their own language. And in addition the Negroes. Very powerful incentives are needed to form a single party out of these elements. There is sometimes a sudden strong elan, but the bourgeoisie need only wait passively, and the dissimilar elements of the working class will fall apart again.
>
> Third. Lastly the protective tariff system must have enabled

the workers to participate in the sort of prosperity which we in Europe (apart from Russia, where, however, not the workers profit from it but the bourgeoisie) have not seen for years.[3]

Engels's point on the impact of the U.S. Constitution—whose elaborate system of checks and balances, and its built-in concern to protect the property rights of wealthy elites, gave it an even more conservatizing force than Engels notes—must be supplemented by points on geography and violence. The United States was, after all, a huge country: a working-class political triumph in this nation would—in terms of land mass—be roughly equivalent to such a triumph from London, Paris, Amsterdam, Lisbon, and Copenhagen all the way into the Russian heartland thousands of miles to the east. Related to this was an immense cultural diversity within the United States—not only between the two coasts, the midwestern heartland, the far west and southwest, but especially between the North and the South. The betrayal of the ex-slaves in the South at the end of the Reconstruction era (1866–1877), thanks to a far-reaching compromise between the post-Civil War upper classes of both regions, created a reactionary enclave in the Southern states overseen by a paternalistic elite, with former slave-owning "Bourbons" of the plantations blending with industrially friendly "Redeemers" willing to cooperate with Northern businessmen. They justified their domination of "the New South" in the name of white power, with a strong conservative-militaristic tradition and undergirded by systematic suppression of democratic rights for blacks, and the utilization of terroristic violence against those perceived as undermining the region's "way of life." In fact, violence was an integral element in the larger historical reality: a systematic destruction and repression against the various Native American peoples ("Indians") who stood in the way of capitalist progress, but also the use of force and violence—sometimes through the use of the police and the army, sometimes through the use of private armies hired by businessmen—to repress the struggles and organizations of workers seeking higher wages, a shorter workday, and dignity on the job and in society. This, in turn, sometimes generated an explosive working-class counterviolence of mass strikes and open rebellions (or sometimes a more covert counterviolence that, in certain circumstances, could all too easily slide into the triumph of organized crime).[4]

The point that Engels makes on immigration is certainly one of the keys to the history of the U.S. working class. This, in turn, involves several realities: a nativist bigotry against the teeming hordes of newcomers, with many native-born workers inclined to exclude foreigners from their workplaces and communities; the willingness of many newly arrived immigrants to accept working conditions and wages vastly inferior to those achieved earlier by American workers; and the difficulty of different groups of workers from linguistically, ethnically, and culturally diverse backgrounds to share a sense of solidarity as part of the same working class. Consequently, workers were effectively pitted against each other to the detriment of all except the employer who profited from his enhanced control over the fragmented work force. And to a large extent, as W. E. B. Du Bois observed in 1903, the problem of the twentieth century would be the problem of the color line. In the United States immigrant groups from various parts of Europe joined with the majority of native-born workers to emphasize their "whiteness," since the presumed racial superiority could be utilized to justify a rich array of legal, material, cultural, and other privileges not extended to the so-called "lesser breeds" of African Americans, Asian Americans,

Latin Americans, and Native Americans. The poisonous impact of ethnic hatreds and pervasive racism—inadequately comprehended by Marx and Aveling in 1886–1887—continues to be felt down to the present day.[5]

Another cleavage within the working class, reflecting centuries-long patriarchal norms, placed women legally, politically, economically, culturally, and psychologically in a subordinate position to men. While Marx and Aveling were avowed supporters of women's rights and, in this study, demonstrate a sensitivity to the plight of women workers, they proved unable to give adequate attention to the myriad forms of special oppression experienced by women in the United States of their time. Complex specifics of the *intersection* of class, racial, and gender identities—and the decisive meaning of this for the experience, consciousness, struggles, and future evolution of the U.S. working class—were generally beyond the grasp of even the most sophisticated nineteenth-century socialists. They have eluded the comprehension of many latter-day Marxists as well.[6]

Less surprising is the relative inattention of Marx and Aveling—aside from brief comments about the Grange—to the rising populist movement among hard-pressed farmers in the South and the Midwest. After all, this was a book about the *working-class* movement (the movement of those whose living was based on the sale of labor-power for wages), whereas the small farmers who formed the populist base have generally been seen as a "petty bourgeois" layer—small-scale land-owners engaged in petty commodity production—destined to be crowded out by larger and more efficient business interests as the capitalist economy continued to develop along lines of growing productivity. The populist revolt against such capitalist progress was seen by many deterministic leftists (and also many influential historians) as "reactionary" by definition. The fact is, however, that in the 1890s a powerful challenge was mounted by these embattled small farmers, in alliance with sections of the labor movement (the Knights of Labor, the American Railway Union, trade-union activists in Chicago and other Midwestern urban areas), and with various radical and maverick currents, to defend democracy (rule by the people) from plutocracy (rule by the rich). This challenge was deflected into the Democratic Party and then decisively crushed by a Republican Party electoral effort that was massively financed by big business interests in the Presidential campaign of 1896. In fact, some Marxist-influenced labor activists of the time scornfully rejected the notion that they should make common cause with the "petty bourgeois" farmers.[7]

What is intriguing is that almost two decades earlier, in a comment to his friend Engels about the violent nationwide labor uprising of 1877, Karl Marx had suggested the possibility of the predominantly white working-class movement merging with struggles of African American agricultural labor in the South (just betrayed by the Republican Party sellout that dismantled Reconstruction) and the hard-pressed small farmers who would eventually spearhead the populist movement. "What do you think of the workers in the United States?" Marx asked, immediately going on to offer his own views: "This first eruption against the oligarchy of associated capital which has arisen since the Civil War will of course be put down, but it could quite well form the starting point for the establishment of a serious labor party in the United States. There are moreover two favorable circumstances," he added. "The policy of the new President [Rutherford B. Hayes] will turn the Negroes into allies of the workers, and the large expropriations of land (especially fertile land) in favor of railway, mining, etc., companies will convert the peasants of the West, who are already very disenchanted, into allies of the workers."[8] This was, however, a fleeting insight in Marx's massive intellectual output. Such fertile speculation about the possibility and desirability of far-reaching social alliances was beyond the range even of his thoughtful daughter in 1887.

The failure of majority sectors of the U.S. laboring population to make common cause enabled political representatives of the big business "robber barons" to divide and conquer the various lower-class challengers, consolidating the control of industrial and financial corporations over the nation's economic development and political life. The Democratic Party—based on an alliance of Southern agrarian interests and political machines catering to immigrant communities in Northern urban centers—claimed to be the party of labor. So did the Republican Party, which favored high tariffs facilitating the forward march of industry that would bring jobs and prosperity for all. And when push came to shove, both were dedicated to the triumph of American capitalism that was making the United States a great world power. As Engels noted in his 1893 comments, the maintenance of the protective tariff system by the Republican Party from the 1860s onward facilitated industrial productivity which, among other things, generated: (a) rising profits for the industrial capitalists, (b) a rising need for industrial labor which yielded relatively high employment and wage rates for workers, and (c) lower prices for consumer goods. The result was, as Engels put it, "the sort of prosperity we in Europe have not seen for years." Ironically, such positive developments also helped to bring on periodic depressions—economic downturns, partly fueled by the spectacular production of goods glutting the market—which saw large-scale business failures and soaring unemployment. The paradox was that even such calamities enabled the more efficient forces among the array of competing business corporations to bring more of the economy under their sway, allowing for more spectacular economic performance as the boom times came around again. Such prosperity was further advanced by overseas economic expansion through the Open Door Policy—backed by "dollar diplomacy" and "gunboat diplomacy"—designed to secure foreign markets, raw materials, and investment opportunities that were vital to the future of America's dynamic market economy.[9]

The overwhelming triumph of corporate capitalism, no less than the ethnic and racial fragmentation of the U.S. working class, had a profound impact on the manner in which the U.S. labor movement was to develop. By the dawn of the twentieth century, the movement which Marx and Aveling had described was separating into increasingly conservatized and radicalized components. The radicals reflected the socialist commitments and inclinations identified in this study, with many "unconscious socialists" (one thinks of Eugene V. Debs, "Big Bill" Haywood, and others) becoming sufficiently conscious to organize the Socialist Party of America (1901) and the Industrial Workers of the World (1905). The conservatives—including some who had also been influenced by socialism—sought to guide organized labor into a "realistic" accommodation with the triumphant capitalist order. Within this order a moderated and narrowly economic "pure and simple" trade unionism might secure, at least for the more skilled and organized sectors of the labor force, better working conditions, a shorter workday, and higher wages at the workplace. Radicals saw this not only as a betrayal of the labor movement's lofty ideals, but also as a short-sighted betrayal of the majority of the less skilled and less organized workers. Such a tension and division in the ranks of labor, never fully resolved one way or the other, has shaped the history of the U.S. working class throughout the twentieth century.

MARXISM AND AMERICAN LABOR

It is not possible to see clearly the coming of this particular radical/conservative split in the observations of Eleanor Marx and Edward Aveling (although they did identify a different one shaping up in the Knights of Labor). Indeed, one of the striking features of this book is the obvious openness to socialist ideas, and what came to be known as "Marxism," among a broad layer of labor activists. The fact is that for many years some of the most prominent representatives of the American labor movement have looked to Karl Marx and his comrade Frederick Engels as being the source of valuable ideas for the working class. This is because they understood that Marx and Engels were not in favor of some kind of dictatorship over the working class (whether by big businessmen or bureaucratic tyrants), but instead were in favor of democracy: they defended the interests of the working class—they wanted workers, the majority class, not the minority of wealthy businessmen, to be in control of society.

Samuel Gompers, a founder and longtime president of the American Federation of Labor (AFL), described Karl Marx as a "genius... [whose] influence contributed to emphasize the necessity for organization of wage-earners in trade unions and the development of economic power prior to efforts to establish labor government through political methods." Marx's influence can be found in the preamble which Gompers and others put forward for the AFL's constitution in 1886: "a struggle is going on in all the nations of the civilized world, between oppressors and the oppressed of all countries, a struggle between the capitalist and the laborer, which grows in intensity from year to year, and will work disastrous results to the toiling millions, if they are not combined for mutual protection and benefit." According to Gompers: "Some of my early shopmates were zealous Socialists of the Marxian school. They were as high-minded a group of idealists as can be found. They were working hard to establish trade unions." Among "the Socialists who were personal students of Karl Marx," Gompers noted, were immigrant workers "who helped to lay the foundation for the American trade union movement. . . . I learned to appreciate these men as friends and to value their counsel."[10] These are things that the elderly Gompers wrote in his autobiography. Long after he became a conservative figure in the labor movement, he retained his respect for Marx!

It is worth noting that many key figures in the history of the U.S. labor movement were similarly influenced by Marx and his cothinkers. Peter J. McGuire, cited as a good friend and a stalwart socialist by Eleanor Marx in the present volume, was a close associate of Gompers and the foremost leader of the Brotherhood of Carpenters, also considered by many to be the "inventor" of Labor Day. Florence Kelley, daughter of a famous Radical Republican Congressman of Pennsylvania, was herself a pioneering social worker and associate of Jane Addams, as well as a labor activist who led successful fights for job-safety and child-labor laws in the nineteenth and early twentieth centuries, and she considered Marx "the great founder of modern scientific political economy," who demonstrated that "the future rests with the working class." David Dubinsky noted that his union, the International Ladies Garment Workers Union, "was the first big union created by [among other political radicals] the disciples of Karl Marx." Similarly, A. Philip Randolph, founder and leader of the Brotherhood of Sleeping Car Porters, remembered his own discovery of Marx's writings as "exciting," because it was like "finally running into an idea which gives you your outlook on life." Militant organizers of the Industrial Workers of the World viewed the writings of Marx and Engels as "part of an education by all progressive-minded Americans," in the words of former IWW spokesperson Elizabeth Gurley Flynn.[11]

Indeed, at the founding convention of the IWW in 1905, Eugene V. Debs, the founder and president of the American Railway Union who became a popular socialist leader, noted: "Karl Marx, the profound economic philosopher, uttered the inspiring shibboleth a half a century ago: 'Workers of all countries unite; you have nothing to lose but your chains. You have a world to gain.'" Elaborating on Marx's thought, Debs continued: "You workers are the only class essential to society; all others can be spared, but without you society would perish. You produce the wealth, you support government, you create and conserve civilization. You ought to be, can be and will be the masters of the earth."[12]

In later years, Marx's influence was strong among many of those who built the unions on which was based the Congress of Industrial Organizations (CIO), and later the AFL-CIO—unions of mine workers and steel workers, garment workers and clothing workers, auto workers and electrical workers, transit workers and teamsters, longshoremen and maritime workers, office workers and hospital workers, teachers and social workers, and many more. Certainly as of the 1990s, a majority of unionized workers have never been socialists in the United States, nor have a majority of AFL-CIO union leaders studied Marx. But this hardly means that ideas associated with Karl Marx are incompatible with or necessarily rejected by the American labor movement. In fact, the history of U.S. labor—reflected in the present volume—demonstrates that such ideas were an integral part of the ferment and forward movement among conscious and organized workers in the United States.[13]

In a left-wing history of U.S. workers that appeared in 1955,

Richard O. Boyer and Herbert M. Morais wrote: "The Chinese ideograph for the word 'crisis' is formed by two characters, one representing 'opportunity,' and the other representing 'danger.' The American labor movement, confronted with world crisis, as is every movement and every person, is faced with danger on one hand and opportunity on the other." Although the authors were referring to the crisis of another time, the U.S. working class has entered a new period of crisis in the 1990s. On the one hand, we see the plummeting of so-called middle-class living standards, the rapid deterioration of the urban environment (not to mention planetary ecology), and the dramatic erosion of democracy in the face of immensely powerful multinational corporations.[14] One aspect of the opportunity we face involves the critical-minded and angry reaction of increasing numbers of people—which could create a powerful impulse to bring society, and the economic resources and structures on which society depends, under the democratic control of its people, for the benefit of all. It is unlikely that such a thing will happen, unless the working-class majority, which involves approximately 80 percent of the U.S. population, becomes determined to make it happen. Volumes such as this may contribute to the realization of the positive element in the present crisis, offering the reader a greater sense of historical perspective: where we have been, where we are, and where we might go.

LEARNING MORE ABOUT WORKING-CLASS HISTORY

There is much more to be learned about the history of the U.S. working class in the late nineteenth century (as well as in earlier and later years) than can be found in the stimulating but modest report of Marx and Aveling. Today's readers who have an interest in this history are fortunate in being able to turn to a considerable amount of material, some of which is referred to in the endnotes of this introduction and elsewhere in this volume. It may be useful to cite additional key works which can provide a framework for continued study. Readers seeking a brief but stimulating single-volume overview of the U.S. working class in the nineteenth century can turn to Bruce Laurie, *Artisans into Workers: Labor in Nineteenth-Century America* (New York: Hill and Wang, 1989). A volume of essays on what happened next is provided by John Hinshaw and Paul Le Blanc, eds., *U.S. Labor in the Twentieth Century* (Amherst, N.Y.: Humanity Books, 2000). Also see Paul LeBlanc, *A Short History of the U.S. Working Class: From Colonial Times to the Twenty-first Century* (Amherst, N.Y.: Humanity Books, 1999).

There are two classic multivolume histories. The first pioneering work, which tends to justify the "pure and simple" trade union approach which became predominant in the AFL, was produced by John R. Commons in association with David J. Saposs, Helen L. Sumner, E. B. Mittelman, H. E. Hoagland, John B. Andrews, Selig Perlman, and Philip Taft, *History of Labor in the United States*, 4 vols. (New York: Macmillan, 1918–1935). The second, produced by Philip S. Foner, *A History of the Labor Movement in the United States*, 10 vols. (New York: International Publishers, 1947–1994), covers much of the same ground, but utilizes an explicitly Marxist orientation and incorporates more recent scholarship and sensibilities—although critics from both the left and the right have identified what they perceive to be limitations in what is, nonetheless, an invaluable resource. These works can be profitably supplemented by older surveys from left-wing participants: Friedrich A. Sorge, *Labor Movement in the United States: A History of the American Working Class from Colonial Times to 1890*, ed. Philip S. Foner and Brewster Chamberlin (Westport, Conn.: Greenwood Press, 1977); *Labor Movement in the United States: A History of the American Working Class from 1890 to 1896*, ed. Kai Schoenhals (Westport, Conn.: Greenwood Press, 1987); and Morris Hillquit, *A History of Socialism in the United States*, 2d ed. (New York: Macmillan, 1909). A critical assessment of the Marx/Sorge influence on U.S. labor is advanced by Timothy Messer-Kruse, *The Yankee International: Marxism and the American Reform Tradition, 1848–1876* (Chapel Hill: University of North Carolina Press, 1998). A scathing critique of ideological narrowness and bureaucratic conservatism in the U.S. labor movement can be found in Paul Buhle, *Taking Care of Business: Samuel Gompers, George Meany, Lane Kirkland, and the Tragedy of American Labor* (New York: Monthly Review Press, 1999).

Essential for those who want to understand the history of the U.S. working class are the contributions of the great "social historians" of U.S. labor, Herbert Gutman and David Montgomery. Gutman's magnificent essays are collected in *Work, Culture, and Society in Industrializing America* (New York: Alfred A. Knopf, 1976), and *Power and Culture, Essays on the American Working Class*, ed. Ira Berlin (New York: Pantheon Books, 1987). Much of Montgomery's fine work can be found in four volumes: *Beyond Equality: Labor and the Radical Republicans, 1862–1872* (New York: Alfred A. Knopf, 1967); *Workers Control in America: Studies in the History of Work* (New York: Cambridge University Press, 1982); *The Fall of the House of Labor: The Workplace, the State, and American Labor Activism, 1865–1925* (New York: Cambridge University Press, 1987); and *Citizen Worker: The Experience of Workers in the United States with Democracy and the Free*

Market During the Nineteenth Century (New York: Cambridge University Press, 1995).

While the story of the American Federation of Labor is amply covered in the Commons and Foner histories, one can also consult: Lewis L. Lorwin, *The American Federation of Labor* (Washington, D.C.: Brookings Institute, 1933); Philip Taft, *The A.F.L. in the Time of Gompers* (New York: Harper, 1957); and Bernard Mandel, *Samuel Gompers, A Biography* (Yellow Springs, Ohio: Antioch Press, 1963). On the Knights of Labor, three additional studies ought to be consulted: Norman Ware, *The Labor Movement in the United States, 1860–1895: A Study in Democracy* (New York: Appleton and Co., 1929); Leon Fink, *Workingmen's Democracy: The Knights of Labor and American Politics* (Urbana: University of Illinois Press, 1983); and Robert E. Weir, *Beyond Labor's Veil: The Culture of the Knights of Labor* (University Park: Pennsylvania State University Press, 1996). A useful history of the struggle for the eight-hour workday is David Roediger and Philip S. Foner, *Our Own Time: A History of American Labor and the Working Day* (London: Verso, 1989). For those U.S. working people who wonder whatever became of the eight-hour workday, two books may be useful: Juliet Schor, *The Overworked American* (New York: Basic Books, 1991), and Michael Yates, *Longer Hours, Fewer Jobs: Employment and Unemployment in the United States* (New York: Monthly Review Press, 1994).

Marxism in the United States is surveyed in Daniel Bell, *Marxian Socialism in the United States* (Princeton: Princeton University Press, 1967) and Paul Buhle, *Marxism in the United States*, rev. ed. (London: Verso, 1991). A useful collection of primary documents can be found in Albert Fried, ed., *Socialism in America From the Shakers to the Third International: A Docu-*

mentary History (Garden City, N.Y.: Anchor Books, 1970). An older study which still has value, dealing both with Marxist and non-Marxist currents in the late nineteenth century, is Howard Quint, *The Forging of American Socialism: Origins of the Modern Movement* (Indianapolis: Bobbs-Merrill, 1964). On the quite significant radical labor movement led by Chicago's so-called anarchists (who had a far more Marxist orientation than is commonly understood), there are five outstanding books: Henry David, *The History of the Haymarket Affair* (New York: Collier, 1963); Paul Avrich, *The Haymarket Tragedy* (Princeton: Princeton University Press, 1984); Bruce Nelson, *Beyond the Martyrs: A Social History of Chicago's Anarchists, 1870–1900* (New Brunswick: Rutgers University Press, 1988); Franklin Rosemont and David Roediger, eds., *Haymarket Scrapbook* (Chicago: Charles H. Kerr Co., 1986); and Philip S. Foner, ed., *The Autobiographies of the Haymarket Martyrs* (New York: Monad Press, 1969). Although mentioned in the endnotes, it is worth directing readers' attention, once again to Mari Jo Buhle, Paul Buhle, and Dan Georgakas, eds., *Encyclopedia of the American Left* (Urbana: University of Illinois Press, 1992).

Aspects of working-class culture are illuminated in many of the works mentioned above, as well as in the following: Roy Rozenzweig, *Eight Hours for What We Will: Workers and Leisure in an Industrial City, 1870–1920* (New York: Cambridge University Press, 1983); Jim Cullen, *The Art of Democracy: A Concise History of Popular Culture in the United States* (New York: Monthly Review Press, 1996); and Lawrence Levine, *The Unpredictable Past: Explorations in American Cultural History* (New York: Oxford University Press, 1993).

The most ambitious recent survey of U.S. working-class history is *Who Built America? Working People and the Nation's Economy, Politics, Culture and Society*, published in two massive pieces: *Volume One: From Conquest and Colonization Through the Great Uprising of 1877*, by Bruce Levine, Stephen Brier, David Brundage, Edward Countryman, Dorothy Fennell, Marcus Rediker (New York: Pantheon Books, 1989), and *Volume Two: From the Gilded Age to the Present*, by Joshua Freeman, Nelson Lichtenstein, Stephen Brier, David Bensman, Susan Porter Benson, David Brundage, Bret Eynon, Bruce Levine, and Bryan Palmer (New York: Pantheon Books, 1992).

It is worth comparing and contrasting the picture presented by Marx and Aveling with the realities of the late twentieth century. In addition to the works of Kim Moody—*An Injury to All: The Decline of American Unionism* (London: Verso, 1988) and *Workers in a Lean World* (London: Verso, 1997)—useful sources include: Andrew Levison, *The Working Class Majority* (New York: Coward, McCann & Geohegan, 1974); Studs Terkel, *Working* (New York: Avon Books, 1975); Charles Spencer, *Blue Collar: An Internal Examination of the Workplace* (Chicago: Lakeside Charter Books, 1977); Harley Shaiken, *Work Transformed: Automation and Labor in the Computer Age* (Lexington, Mass.: Lexington Books/D. C. Heath and Co., 1986); Patricia Cayo Sexton, *The War on Labor and the Left: Understanding America's Unique Conservatism* (Boulder, Colo.: Westview Press, 1991); Martin Glaberman and Seymour Faber, *Working for Wages: The Roots of Insurgency* (Dix Hills, N.Y.: General Hall, 1998); Ellen Meiksins Wood, Peter Meiksins, and Michael D. Yates, eds., *Rising from the Ashes? Labor in the Age of "Global" Capitalism* (New York: Monthly Review Press, 1999). A short, readable, fact-filled resource is Michael Yates's *Why Unions Matter* (New York: Monthly Review Press, 1998).

FINAL NOTES AND ACKNOWLEDGEMENTS

The Working-Class Movement in America, written in 1887 after the 1886 U.S. tour of Eleanor Marx and Edward Aveling, was first published in 1888 by Swan Sonnenschein and Company (London), with a second enlarged edition (the basis for the present volume) appearing in 1891.

Thanks are due to Scott McLemee for assistance in retyping. At least some typographical errors and some archaic spellings or punctuations have been eliminated, and a few editor's footnotes have been added to clarify points made in the text. Thanks are due to Dr. Csaba Toth, Chair of the History Department at Carlow College, for support and suggestions, and to Dr. David Dixon of Slippery Rock University's History Department for an especially helpful reference. Dr. Elaine Bernard of the Harvard Trade Union Program raised interesting challenges on aspects of the Marx-Aveling work which helped to move my own thinking forward. Dr. Carol McAllister, associated with the Graduate School of Public Health and the Anthropology Department of the University of Pittsburgh, has been an especially important friend for many years, and her influence has helped to shape some of what I have written here.

There are many in the early twenty-first century who follow in the footsteps of the authors of this book, as well as the footsteps of those who are cited and quoted as explaining and struggling against the oppression of U.S. working class. Among the many are dedicated activists who write for, edit, and produce the invaluable monthly publication *Labor Notes*, which provides sometimes depressing, sometimes exciting, and always readable and informative accounts of what is going on in workplaces, in unions, and in the working class as a whole in the United States (and sometimes elsewhere). It only makes sense, therefore, that all royalties from this book go to *Labor Notes*. Readers who want to compare the working-class movement in America in the 1880s with that of today may wish to subscribe to this vital monthly (only $20.00 per year), which can be obtained by writing to *Labor Notes*, 7435 Michigan Avenue, Detroit, Michigan 48210.

NOTES

1. For a discussion of Marxism's historical evolution, see my own *From Marx to Gramsci: A Reader in Revolutionary Marxist Politics* (Atlantic Highlands, N.J.: Humanities Press, 1996). Leon Samson's ideas are presented in *Toward a United Front* (New York: Farrar and Rinehart, 1935) and analyzed in John H. M. Laslett and Seymour Martin Lipset, eds., *Failure of a Dream? Essays in the History of American Socialism* (Garden City, N.Y.: 1974), pp. 70–72, 443–62. Relevant works of the 1950–1960 period include: Daniel Boorstin, *The Genius of American Politics* (Chicago: University of Chicago Press, 1953); Louis Hartz, *The Liberal Tradition in America* (New York: Harcourt, Brace and World, 1955); Seymour Martin Lipset, *Political Man* (Garden City, N.Y.: Anchor Books, 1963); Daniel Bell, *The End of Ideology* (New York: Free Press, 1960); Chaim Waxman, ed., *The End of Ideology Debate* (New York: Funk and Wagnalls, 1968); C. L. R. James, *American Civilization* (Cambridge, Mass.: Blackwell, 1993). Also see John P. Diggins, *The Rise and Fall of the American Left* (New York: W. W. Norton, 1992), pp. 187–217; Richard H. Pells, *The Liberal Mind in a Conservative Age: American Intellectuals in the 1940s and 1950s* (New York: Harper and Row, 1985), pp. 130–62; and Kent Worcester, *C. L. R. James: A Political Biography* (Albany: State University of New York Press, 1996), pp. 103–15. Themes touched on in the following paragraph are discussed more thoroughly in Paul Le Blanc, "Culture, Identity, Class Struggle: Practical Critique of the Discourse on Post-Marxism," *Transformation* 1 (spring 1995): 290–301.

2. Marx and Engels, "Manifesto of the Communist Party," in Le Blanc, *From Marx to Gramsci*, p. 130; Melvyn Dubofsky, *Industrialism and the American Worker, 1865–1920* (Arlington Heights, Ill.: AHM Publishing Corp., 1975), p. 3.

3. Nelly Rumyantseva, ed., *Marx and Engels on the United States* (Moscow: Progress Publishers, 1979), pp. 284, 333–34.

4. Howard Zinn capably discusses and sifts through controversies on the U.S. Constitution in a volume well worth consulting on various aspects of American history, *A People's History of the United States* (New York: Harper and Row, 1980), pp. 89–101, but also see Edward Countryman, *The American Revolution* (New York: Hill and Wang, 1985), and Jules Lobel, ed., *A Less Than Perfect Union: Alternative Perspectives on the U.S. Constitution* (New York: Monthly Review Press, 1988). Classic studies of the Reconstruction betrayal and its meaning can be found in W. E. B. Du Bois, *Black Reconstruction in America, 1860–1880* (New York: Atheneum 1985); Eric Foner, *Reconstruction: America's Unfinished Revolution, 1863–1877* (New York: Harper and Row, 1988); and C. Van Woodward, *The Origins of the New South, 1877–1913* (Baton Rouge: Louisiana University Press, 1951). A fine account of the war against the Indians is Dee Brown, *Bury My Heart at Wounded Knee* (New York: Bantam Books, 1972); see also Francis Jennings, *The Founders of America: From the Earliest Migrations to the Present* (New York: W.W. Norton, 1994). Louis Adamic's *Dynamite: The Story of Class Violence in America* (New York: Viking, 1934) provides a significant analysis, which can be usefully supplemented by the later scholarship of Robert Justin Goldstein, *Political Repression in Modern America, 1870 to the Present* (New York: Schenkman Publishing Co., 1978); the points about labor gangsterism, raised in Adamic, are elaborated in Harold Seidman, *Labor Czars: A History of Labor Racketeering* (New York: Liveright Publishing Corp., 1938). An impressive synthesis of U.S. historical development from 1890 to 1940 can be found in Alan Dawley, *Struggles for Justice: Social Responsibility and the Liberal State* (Cambridge: Harvard University Press, 1991).

5. The outstanding account of the multicultural experience of American history is Ronald Takaki's *A Different Mirror: A History of Multicultural America* (Boston: Little, Brown and Co., 1993). Other valuable contributions include: Isaac A. Hourwich, *Immigration and Labor* (New York: Macmillan, 1912); John Higham, *Strangers in the Land: Patterns of American Nativism, 1860–1925*, 2d ed. (New Brunswick: Rutgers University Press, 1988); David Brody, *Steelworkers in America: The Nonunion Era* (New York: Harper and Row, 1969); John Bodnar, *The Transplanted: A History of Immigrants in Urban America* (Bloomington: Indiana University Press, 1987); and Dirk Hoerder, ed., *American Labor and Immigration History, 1877–1920s: European Research* (Urbana: University of Illinois Press, 1983). Marc Karson's *American Labor Unions and Politics, 1900–1918* (Boston: Beacon Press, 1965) identifies a serious religious-cultural fissure that pitted Catholics against socialists, which also helped to fragment the labor movement. Aspects of the effects of racism in U.S. history (including in U.S. labor) are explored in: W. E. B. Du Bois, *The Souls of Black Folk* (New York: New American Library, 1969); C. Van Woodward, *The Strange Career of Jim Crow*, 3d ed. (New York: Oxford University Press, 1974); Julius Jacobson, ed., *The Negro and the American Labor Movement* (Garden City, N.Y.: Anchor Books, 1968); August Meier and Elliott Rudwick, *From Plantation to Ghetto*, 3d ed. (New York: Hill and Wang, 1976); Philip S. Foner, *Organized Labor and the Black Worker 1619–1981* (New York: International Publishers, 1981); Philip S. Foner and Ronald L. Lewis, eds., *Black Workers: A Documentary History from Colonial Times to the Present* (Philadelphia: Temple University Press, 1989); Manning Marable, *How Capitalism Underdeveloped Black America* (Boston: South End Press, 1983); Alexander Saxton, *The Indispensable Enemy, Labor and the Anti-Chinese Movement in California* (Berkeley: University of California Press, 1971); Alexander Saxton, *The Rise and Fall of the White Republic: Class Politics and Mass Culture in Nineteenth-Century America* (London: Verso, 1990); David Roediger, *The Wages of Whiteness: Race and the Making of the American Working Class* (London: Verso, 1991).

6. General discussions of the oppression and struggles of women in the nineteenth century can be found in Sheila Rowbotham, *Women, Resistance, and Revolution* (New York: Vintage Books, 1974); Eleanor Flexner, *A Century of Struggle: The Women's Rights Movement in the United States* (Cambridge: Harvard University Press, 1959); and Miriam Schneir, ed., *Feminism: The Essential Historical Writings* (New York: Random House, 1972). Valuable explorations of women in the history of the U.S. working class and labor movement are available in Barbara Mayer Wertheimer, *We Were There: The Story of Working Women in America* (New York: Pantheon Books, 1977); Philip S. Foner, *Women and the American Labor Movement: From the First Trade Unions to the Present* (New York: The Free Press, 1982); Alice Kessler-Harris, *Out to Work: A History of Wage-Earning Women in America* (New York: Oxford University Press, 1982); Meredith Tax, *The Rising of the Women* (New York: Monthly Review Press, 1980); Rosalyn Baxandall, Linda Gordon, and Susan Reverby, eds., *America's Working Women: A Documentary History—1600 to the Present* (New York: Vintage Books, 1976). Especially useful for considering the intersection of class, race, and gender are Karen Brodkin Sacks, "Toward a Unified Theory of Race, Class, and Gender," *American Ethnologist* 16, no. 3 (1989): 534–50; and Vicki L. Ruiz and Ellen Carol DuBois, eds., *Unequal Sisters: A Multicultural Reader in U.S. Women's History*, 2d ed. (New York Routledge, 1994).

7. Judgments of mainstream historians are to be found in Richard Hofstadter, *The Age of Reform: From Bryan to F.D.R.* (New York: Alfred A Knopf, 1955); Samuel Hays, *The Response to Industrialism, 1885–1914* (Chicago: Chicago University Press, 1957); Robert H. Wiebe, *The Search for Order, 1877–1920* (New York: Hill and Wang, 1967). Important studies more sympathetic to the populist challenge are: John D. Hicks, *The Populist Revolt* (Minneapolis: University of Minnesota Press, 1931); Norman Pollack, *The Populist Response to Industrial America* (Cambridge: Harvard University Press, 1967); and Lawrence Goodwyn, *Democratic Promise: The Populist Movement in America* (New York: Oxford University Press, 1976). The Populists speak for

themselves in Norman Pollack, ed., *The Populist Mind* (Indianapolis: Bobbs-Merrill, 1967). On the earlier agrarian movement, the Patrons of Husbandry, better known as the Grange, see Solon J. Buck's classic, *The Granger Movement* (Cambridge: Harvard University Press, 1913).

8. Rumyantseva, *Marx and Engels on the United States*, p. 272.

9. Two invaluable studies on U.S. economic development are Louis M. Hacker, *The Triumph of American Capitalism* (New York: Simon and Schuster, 1940); and Paul Baran and Paul Sweezy, *Monopoly Capital, An Essay on the American Economic and Social Order* (New York: Monthly Review Press, 1968). Alfred Chandler's *The Visible Hand: The Managerial Revolution in American Business* (Cambridge: Harvard University Press, 1977) focuses on organizational developments. The interrelationship of capitalism's organizational evolution and the sometimes hidden, sometimes open struggle between workers and their employers is discussed in two studies with similar and yet somewhat different perspectives: Harry Braverman's classic *Labor and Monopoly Capital: The Degradation of Work in the Twentieth Century* (New York: Monthly Review Press, 1976); and David M. Gordon, Richard Edwards, and Michael Reich, *Segmented Work, Divided Workers: The Historical Transformation of Labor in the United States* (Cambridge: Cambridge University Press, 1982). Economic expansionism is traced in Scott Nearing and Joseph Freeman, *Dollar Diplomacy: A Study in American Imperialism* (New York: B. W. Huebsch and Viking Press, 1926); William Appleman Williams, *The Tragedy of American Diplomacy*, new ed. (New York: W. W. Norton, 1988); and Harry Magdoff, *Imperialism: From the Colonial Age to the Present* (New York: Monthly Review Press, 1978). Valuable studies of economic, political, and ideological developments in this period are treated respectively in Matthew Josephson's two studies, *The Robber Barons: The Great American Capitalists, 1861–1901* (New York: Harcourt, Brace and World, 1934) and *The Politicos, 1865–1896* (New York: Harcourt, Brace and World, 1938); and Robert McClosky's *American Conservatism in the Age of Enterprise, 1865–1910* (New York: Harper and Row, 1964). Also see the remarkably

radical analysis of a former U.S. Senator from South Dakota in R. F. Pettigrew, *Imperial Washington: The Story of American Public Life from 1870 to 1920* (Chicago: Charles H. Kerr, 1922). Brilliant case-studies of the economic, political, and cultural impact of the corporations' expanding and deepening power in the face of working-class resistance are offered by Francis G. Couvares, *The Remaking of Pittsburgh: Class and Culture in an Industrializing City, 1877–1919* (Albany: State University of New York Press, 1982); and Paul Krause, *The Battle for Homestead 1880–1892, Politics, Culture, and Steel* (Pittsburgh: University of Pittsburgh Press, 1992).

10. Samuel Gompers, *Seventy Years of Life and Labor*, vol. 1 (New York: E. P. Dutton and Co., 1926), pp. 51, 381; "The AFL, 1886 Preamble," Albert Fried, ed., *Except to Walk Free: Documents and Notes in the History of American Labor* (Garden City, N.Y.: Anchor Books, 1974), p. 153. Also worth examining are Stuart B. Kaufman, *Samuel Gompers and the Origins of the American Federation of Labor 1848–1896* (Westport, Conn.: Greenwood Press, 1973), and Philip S. Foner, *The Workingmen's Party of the United States: A History of the First Marxist Party in the Americas* (Minneapolis: MEP Publications, 1984).

11. Florence Kelley, *The Autobiography of Florence Kelley: Notes of Sixty Years*, ed. Kathryn Kish Sklar (Chicago: Charles H. Kerr Co., 1986), pp. 102, 103; David Dubinsky and A. H. Raskin, *David Dubinsky: A Life With Labor* (New York: Simon and Schuster, 1977), p. 57; Jervis Anderson, *A. Philip Randolph: A Biographical Portrait* (New York: Harcourt, Brace, Jovanovich, 1973), p. 62; Elizabeth Gurley Flynn, *I Speak My Own Piece: Autobiography of "The Rebel Girl"* (New York: Masses and Mainstream, 1955), p. 41. For a tragic portrait of P. J. McGuire—which mistakenly identifies him as a "Lassallean" (which he himself never did) but sharply traces the overwhelming of his glowing socialist commitments by his later tactical acceptance of "pure and simple" trade unionism—see Robert A. Christie's valuable study *Empire in Wood: A History of the Carptenters' Union* (Ithaca: Cornell University, 1956).

12. Eugene V. Debs, "Industrial Unionism," in *Writings and*

Speeches of Eugene V. Debs, ed. Joseph M. Bernstein (New York: Hermitage Press, 1948), p. 235.

13. Popular histories documenting the Marxist influence in the U.S. labor movement include Sidney Lens, *Radicalism in America* (New York: Thomas Y. Crowell, 1969); Thomas R. Brooks, *Toil and Trouble: A History of American Labor* (New York: Dell Publishing Co., 1971); James R. Green, *The World of the Worker: Labor in the Twentieth Century* (New York: Hill and Wang, 1980). A number of case studies are presented in John H. M. Laslett's *Labor and the Left: A Study of Socialist and Radical Influences in the American Labor Movement, 1881–1924* (New York: Basic Books, 1970). A profound sense of 1930s and 1940s labor radicalism—conveyed by skilled labor journalists who were participant-observers—can be found in Art Preis, *Labor's Giant Step: Twenty Years of the CIO* (New York: Pathfinder Press, 1972) and Len DeCaux, *Labor Radical: From the Wobblies to the CIO: A Personal History* (Boston: Beacon Press, 1970). A far-ranging survey is offered in Staughton Lynd, ed., *American Labor Radicalism: Testimonies and Interpretations* (New York: John Wiley and Sons, 1973). More detailed explorations can be found in Mary Jo Buhle, Paul Buhle, and Dan Georgakas, eds., *Encyclopedia of the American Left* (Urbana: University of Illinois Press, 1992) and in Melvyn Dubofsky and Warren Van Tine, eds., *Labor Leaders in America* (Urbana: University of Illinois Press, 1987). Considerably more detail on specifics in the 1930s and 1940s can be found in: Steven Fraser, *Labor Shall Rule: Sidney Hillman and the Rise of American Labor* (New York: Free Press, 1991); Joshua B. Freeman, *In Transit: The Transit Workers Union in New York City, 1933–1966* (New York: Oxford University Press, 1989); Ronald W. Schatz, *The Electrical Workers: A History of Labor at General Electric and Westinghouse, 1923-60* (Urbana: University of Illinois Press, 1983); Nelson Lichtenstein, *The Most Dangerous Man in Detroit: Walter Reuther and the Fate of American Labor* (New York: Basic Books, 1996); Farrell Dobbs, *Teamster Rebellion* (New York: Monad Press, 1972), *Teamster Power* (New York: Monad Press, 1973), *Teamster Politics* (New York: Monad

Press, 1975), *Teamster Bureaucracy* (New York: Monad Press, 1977); Charles P. Larrow, *Harry Bridges: The Rise and Fall of Radical Labor in the U.S.*, 2d ed. (Westport, Conn.: Lawrence Hill, 1977). Efforts to place this all in analytical context can be found in David Saposs, *Left-Wing Unionism: A Study of Radical Policies and Tactics* (New York: International Publishers, 1926); C. Wright Mills, *The New Men of Power: America's Labor Leaders* (New York: Harcourt, Brace and Co., 1948); and Simeon Larson and Bruce Nissen, eds., *Theories of the Labor Movement* (Detroit: Wayne University Press, 1987).

14. Richard O. Boyer and Herbert M. Morais, *Labor's Untold Story* (New York: Cameron Associates, 1955), pp. 378–79. The crisis of which they spoke involved the dangers associated with the Cold War (the threat of nuclear annihilation and the problem of what President Dwight D. Eisenhower later labeled the "military-industrial complex") and the opportunities generated by the high productive level of the U.S. economy, which—then as now—had the potential for creating a good life for all people. Aspects of the current crisis are laid out quite clearly in two decidedly nonleftist, but challenging and fact-filled accounts: Paul Kennedy, *Preparing for the Twenty-first Century* (New York: Random House, 1993), and Kevin Phillips, *The Politics of Rich and Poor: Wealth and the American Electorate in the Reagan Aftermath* (New York: Harper Collins, 1991). Also see essential works by Kim Moody, *An Injury to All: The Decline of American Unionism* (London: Verso, 1988), and *Workers in a Lean World* (London: Verso, 1997).

Essay
On the Uses of Eleanor Marx
by Lisa Frank

It is unfortunate, if unsurprising, that Eleanor Marx is most often remembered for the manner of her death. Here is what we know: on the morning of March 31, 1898, she sent her servant Gertrude Gentry to the pharmacist to procure chloroform and a lethal dose of prussic acid. Within forty minutes of Gertrude's return, Eleanor was dead, a "suicide laboring under mental derangement," at the age of forty-three.

Eleanor Marx, whose life represents a remarkable and indeed unparalleled career of political and intellectual exploration and achievement, would perhaps know why our stories about her tend to dwell on her suicide. More than any of Marx's children, Eleanor shouldered the task of interpreting and expanding her father's legacy and came to understand the politics of memory.[1] In addition to handling Mohr's posthumous accounts,[2] she organized any number of public memorials to dead comrades in arms.[3] She spent hours in the British Museum, assembling documentary evidence for her father's works, unearthing lessons from the past, and learning to contest contemporary historiography.[4] Deeply committed to the working class and socialist movements of her time, Eleanor inhabited a landscape strewn with signifying corpses: Chartists, 48ers, Communards, Fenians, the Haymarket martyrs, the starvelings of London's East End, the hollow women of America's sweatshops, the victims of Bloody Sunday, the dissolved body First International, the desiccated carcass of the Knights of Labor. A whole dead past weighed like a nightmare on the brains of the living, and it was Eleanor's task, as it had been Marx's, to conduct the inquest on behalf of those sacrificed, to elaborate the science of a killing world, and to take issue with those who would, for all-too-interested reasons, account injustice and brutality the natural order of things.

For Eleanor Marx, only socialism—with its insistence on humanity's historical and social being—could provide an adequate worldly forensics. More importantly, only socialism—with its promise of a world organized around and through human equality and self-determination—could redeem the memory of those felled in the struggle within and against the capitalist order. Thus, even if Eleanor would have understood posterity's interest in her premature death (in her earliest treatise-length publication, *The Woman Question*, Eleanor herself speculates on the causes of female suicides[5]), she would have been enraged by many of the more widely circulated accounts.[6]

Lewis S. Feuer's lurid and credulous chapter on Eleanor in *Marx and the Intellectuals* is wholly fixated on her suicide, which on his interpretation is the all but inevitable consequence of a Marxist education:

Her father's teaching left her unprepared for the problem of life. ... The Marxian upbringing itself had produced this apotheosis of self-immolation; the Marxian ethic in practice had negated itself. The ideological way of life left a gaping vacancy in Eleanor's existence. . . . Eleanor Marx's suicide in a blunt way refuted her father's ethic, for Marxism, defining freedom as the recognition of necessity, saw it as achieved when one worked as an appendage to the class struggle for the abolition of classes. The coroner's judgment was that Eleanor Marx had committed suicide while temporarily insane. Eleanor might have answered that her death was a redemptive act of sanity after years immersed in the insane.[7]

Feuer's essay is patently anti-Marxist, and we might expect, if not forgive, the fallacies, dishonesties, and sheer venom needed to make his interpretation appear plausible.[8] Less hostile but nonetheless problematical are the still standard *socialist* narratives (originating, of course, with the leading socialists of Eleanor's time, which is to say, with men) that charge Eleanor's death to Edward Aveling, the monster who reduced her, or so the stories go, to poverty, or desperation, or both.[9]

Aveling's infidelity and profligacy have become legendary, and there can be no doubt that his indifference as a lover and his social indiscretions caused Eleanor both embarrassment and grief. This much is established by Eleanor's correspondence and by credible accounts from a variety of witnesses. Edward was undoubtedly a dislikeable specimen of humanity—much of literary and a not insignificant portion of socialist London detested him—though he was also, Engels and Eleanor excepted, England's most knowledgeable and devoted exponent of Marxian socialism.[10] He was bad with money, but the Avelings lived mainly within their means, which until Engels' death were slim indeed. No charge of financial wrongdoing against Edward was ever proved;[11] indeed, his reputation as a socialist swindler became established only after Eleanor's death. The first wife he reputedly married for her money in fact had very little; the funds he allegedly bilked out of the American Socialist Labor Party were in fact all accounted for; the shillings and pounds he habitually borrowed from acquaintances were in all likelihood never repaid, but his consumptive excesses seem to have been confined to theater tickets, the odd bottle of sherry, or an occasional cigar.

By 1898 Eleanor was well accustomed to Edward's faults; she'd survived them for more than a decade. This is perhaps the reason why sympathetic accounts are unwilling to stop with Edward's real shortcomings. From the time of Eleanor's death, Edward was accused of much worse—of blackmailing Eleanor; of cheating her out of Engels' estate and thus reducing her to poverty; of conspiring with Eleanor's solicitor to suppress her last will and testament, from which, it is supposed, Aveling had been cut; and of initiating a suicide pact from which he sneakily withdrew. But unlike those who seek some special cause for Eleanor's penury, and who provide us with image after poignant image of her dull surrounds—the bric-a-brac furniture, the last crumb of seed-cake—Eleanor Marx herself did not expect that one could both work for wages and live the life of the haute bourgeoisie.[12] She did not take especial delight in the condition to which she was often reduced, but neither did she see it as an unusual tragedy, as if she, alone amongst the many women who struggled to keep the wolf from the door, deserved better. And while there is no question that the frequent faithlessness of Edward Aveling was a source of sorrow to her—his secret marriage to Eva Frye just before their deaths must have shocked even an Edward-inured Eleanor—his affairs were by no means unusual, except perhaps in their fruitlessness. By nineteenth-century standards (which Marx, incidentally, was better at upholding), the complete absence of illegitimate and unsupported children left in Aveling's wake is perhaps most remarkable.[13] To be sure, Aveling was a cad. But he was an ordinary cad. Attributing Eleanor's death to him is both inaccurate and too convenient, for if in fact the threat of poverty and heartache finally broke her, the first was not Edward's doing and the second was scarcely exceptional. Eleanor herself never tolerated great man (or evil man) theories of history. And the suggestion implicit in these accounts is that some (*any*) other man would have been more nurturing—would, in fact, have changed history. The thought might have made Eleanor laugh. Like her father, she could spot the old Peter-Paul shuffle, and like her father, she found hypocrisy amusing.[14]

It is tempting to speculate that had Eleanor been a man, or had she lived in a society that rendered women less socially and economically vulnerable, her life would have ended differently. That her career as a socialist was inseparable from her sex is certainly indisputable. On the occasion of her birth, Marx wrote Frederick Engels to announce the arrival of "a *bona fide* traveler," meaning one who, by law, cannot be refused sustenance and lodging. "Unfortunately," he continued, Eleanor was "of the *sexe par excellence*. Had it been a male the matter would be more acceptable."[15]

Engels in his turn would likewise lament the absence of a suitable male heir. Though much of the last years of his life were anxiously spent preparing for the transfer of Marx's political and theoretical estate, Engels, it appears, never considered Eleanor an appropriate executrix.[16] Despite his deep admiration for the enormous practical and theoretical headway she had made, despite his justifiably grave doubts about each of the male candidates, and despite both his own and Marx's fleeting recognition of Eleanor's qualifications for the post (Marx, for instance, famously remarked that while his eldest daughter Jenny was most like him, Eleanor simply *was* him), she was unaccountably and yet naturally overlooked in most discussions concerning socialist leadership or the socialist movement's major projects.[17]

Not that she didn't lead, nor did she shy away from big projects. At forty, Eleanor was by all accounts *the* foremost British authority on socialist politics abroad (and thus was contributing scores of reports on the progress of various parties and movements to a variety of congresses, papers, and journals). She was unique in her linguistic abilities (and thus was translating, always translating: the speeches of delegates to the Second International, the appeals of linguistic minorities, the work of Ibsen, Lissagary's fine history of the Commune, Plekhanov's *Anarchism and Socialism*). She was, above all, wildly popular (and thus was endlessly orating, at the invitation of scads of unions, political clubs, socialist societies, at demonstration after demonstration, often taking on Aveling's commitments when he was too ill to meet them himself). Almost single-handedly she had forged fragile bonds of trust and solidarity between England's "New Unionists"[18] and revolutionary socialists. Her tactical sense and feel for the struggle were matched only by those of the General himself. And yet, within the circle of socialists who knew her father, she never ceased to be "Tussy," Marx's little minx.

What access Eleanor had to the worlds and knowledges of men—and by any standards, those of her day, or those of our own, her access was extraordinary—she appeared to regard as unremarkable. She was often the sole and the first, but she wore her exceptionalism lightly. Conversely, there is no evidence that Eleanor resented her exclusions from male-dominated socialist circles, though she did complain, to her sisters, about the lack of attention given to her schooling. Characteristically, Eleanor saw in her own situation the effects of broader social forces. Her severe anxieties about finding meaningful work and economic security she approached in historical and political terms: what sorts of employment were open to the daughters of the (financially embarassed) bourgeoisie? How did the restrictions on women's political participation make themselves felt in her own life? How did these restrictions resemble, or differ from, those placed upon the propertyless classes in general? How could we, collectively, expand and improve the choices available to the relatively powerless?[19] The "woman question" was, for Eleanor, just one way of putting the "social question." When female sweet makers organized for better wages and conditions, she viewed their struggles and successes as she would those of any workers. She was genuinely unsurprised by female competence and courage. Analyzing the worlds of the *sexe par excellence*, she submitted her bills on behalf of women in particular but she submitted them to humane society as such.

Indeed, Eleanor's constituency was always this historically *immanent* humanity, the self-conscious proletariat. Her political judgment evolved in relation to a world which had yet to be made and which nonetheless had to be anticipated. Her thinking was of necessity dialectical. When addressing herself to the labor movement, she remained implacably opposed to any version of the family wage, which might prop up living standards of certain sectors of the workforce but which constituted a threat both to the emancipation of women and to the independence of the working class as a whole.[20] Conversely, she voiced serious misgivings about feminisms that failed to grapple with class. She supported the democratic demand for female suffrage and lent her support to those who agitated for it, but she expected little from radical movements led by the bourgeoisie; sooner or later bourgeoisie women would (and did) stumble over their investments in the capitalist system, offering utopias which simply failed to move the masses or becoming genuinely reactionary.[21] And yet, she did not make the common mistake of segregating political demands into those which properly concerned workers and those which were merely "bourgeois." Indeed, she reserved her most bitter vituperation for those socialist colleagues who opposed compulsory schooling, the extension of the franchise, and eight-hours legislation on the grounds that they represented reformist compromise with bourgeois politics and culture. She did not imagine that socialists were inoculated against strategic and tactical error; Henry Hyndman (founder of the Social Democratic Federation) was not, for all his socialism, less prone to bourgeois nationalist myopics. And workers, despite their common exploitation, were not exempted from the struggle to understand and overcome long histories of oppression with deep roots in race, nationality, or gender.[22] In short, Eleanor saw existing movements, demands, and institutions as provisional way-stations on the road to socialism, to be engaged with the utmost seriousness but to be criticized and transformed from the perspective of the future. Again and again Eleanor applauded and looked forward to the making of what she called solidarity from the "ground up," arguing that any institutionalized division between the world's exploited masses must ultimately benefit the guardians of capital. She rarely lost sight of the practical and theoretical obstacles to working-class unification. In her estimation, they were formidable indeed. Women's emancipation, she believed, would require the careful coordination of "coed" unions and parties with campaigns and caucuses in which women took the lead, for their material and political situation warranted separate analysis and necessitated a distinctively female self-emancipation. Working-class solidarity demanded of its theorists and practitioners exceptional clarity and exceptional patience.

Eleanor had these qualities in abundance. She was quick to take the temper of an audience: unlike Aveling, who never deviated from any announced program, Eleanor often noted of the concerns animating her listeners and devised an impromptu address. She was prepared to tinker and to make detours, contorting German grammar to help narrow the gap between that tongue and the Yiddish ears of London's East Enders; later she undertook to study Yiddish in earnest. The politics of the quotidian and the quotidian of politics were her strengths. It was Eleanor who thought to organize children's picnics, providing a limited form of socialist daycare and allowing parents to concentrate more fully on the day's adult agenda. Attending a meeting of a branch of the Shop Assistants' Union, she cheered a resolution to issue a handbill calling for a boycott of those shopkeepers who refused to implement the eight-hour day, and then quietly suggested that for the word boycott—the advocacy of which was then an indictable offense—the unionists substitute the parliamentary phrase "exclusive dealing." Against the temper of the times and the tempers of her colleagues, Eleanor voiced a consistent skepticism about what she, in her correspondence with Laura, referred to as the "Revolution with a very big 'R.' "[23]

Whether Eleanor's admirable feel for the unevenness of proletarian terrain, her fine organizational imagination, and her sheer good sense can be understood as part of a gendered legacy is a matter of opinion. But she grasped what her contemporaries in the unions, the labor parties, and in socialist or feminist currents of her (or our) time saw only dimly: that women, immigrants, the unskilled, were not merely organizable, but were excellent candidates for political and industrial militancy. They were "unconscious socialists," tuned into history's revolutionary frequency. Whether conscious socialists could themselves offer decent programming was, with Eleanor, always a matter open to debate.

There were occasions when Eleanor's sympathy for the oppressed, particularly women, failed to transcend sentimentality; her unflagging benevolence sometimes disguised political and analytical lapses. Though she rarely followed Aveling in his more flamboyant displays of outrage on behalf of women (at the first conference of the Socialist League, he "commented" on the situation of working-class prostitutes by shouting, "I wonder at times how you working men can restrain yourselves from seizing the representatives of the capitalist classes and breaking their necks on the nearest curbstone!"), she could be baited by scandalized genteel sensibility. During the course of the Silvertown strike, women collecting for the relief fund were rumored to be prostitutes. Eleanor believed this to be slander, broadcast in order to antagonize public opinion. But she could do no better than to simply deny the charge in the most moralizing of terms: she never met "more self-respecting factory girls" than those on strike at Silvertown. At the same meeting which occasioned Aveling's outburst, Eleanor produced a similarly purblind "defense" of working girls: "The fact is," she declared, "women are driven to prostitution.... [At current wage rates] nearly all women obliged to earn a living have to choose between starvation and prostitution and this must go on so long as one class can buy the bodies of another, whether in the form of labor power or sexual embraces." Actually, the fact is that many women had (and have) to choose not between prostitution and starvation, but between prostitution and onerous domestic service, between prostitution and abusive household situations, between prostitution and wage work providing less flexibility or time with children, in short, between prostitution and some other not wholly dissimilar point on what we might term the sex-work continuum. Eleanor was surely correct in perceiving important links between prostitutes and other workers and in insisting that women workers are in many ways exemplary proletarians (etymologically, the proletariat is that class which contributes nothing but offspring to the state). But her implicit appeal to ideal forms of sexual congress, grounded, one supposes, in love and family, not only betrayed her ignorance of prostitutes' immediate needs (for decriminalization and unionization), but carried with it the unmistakable odor of bourgeois moralism. Having occupied her own set of compromised and imperfect financial and sexual positions, she ought to have known her allies better.

Eleanor Marx's political and intellectual career began in earnest only after Marx's death in 1883, and her American tour, from which the present volume derives, marks an important turning point in that career. In 1883, Eleanor had been scheduled to accompany German socialist leader Wilhelm Liebknecht on an earlier Socialist Labor Party tour, acting as his secretary. Political developments in Germany forced Liebknecht to cancel.[24] Traveling in 1886 as Aveling's wife, Eleanor exchanged explicit subordination to a paternal colleague (and, it should be added, Party financing) for the position and billing she would retain through her adulthood. Eleanor would find what political independence and maturity she did as Mrs. Marx-Aveling.[25]

The postponement of the tour was a lucky thing, both for Eleanor and for us. Describing America in 1886, *The Working-Class Movement in America* affords a look at the highpoint of the eight-hour movement and at that rarest of American labor events, the general strike. She encountered the Knights of Labor in its heyday, glimpsed the world which gave rise to the AFL, and witnessed the American working class' experimentation with independent political parties in cities across the country. 1886 was a year fraught with possibility and danger, a good year, in other words, to be a socialist. Not only would the socialist platform be relatively congenial to masses of people with experience in bitter industrial struggle, but the revolutionary message of the *Communist Manifesto* would reach people who had more than abstract acquaintance with the *political* questions that their struggle had engendered.

The Avelings' itinerary was ambitious. During their fifteen-week stay, they visited over forty cities, making their way from New York northward through the mill towns of New England, then westward through Buffalo, Milwaukee, Chicago, and Minneapolis. The return leg of their journey encompassed Kansas City, St. Louis, Pittsburgh, and Baltimore. At each stop, they played to packed halls, addressing crowds that numbered in the hundreds and thousands (and, as the Avelings note, "in many places, hundreds were unable to gain admission"). In most cities, their appearances were noted not only by the labor press, but often by the bourgeois dailies. Writing to her sister while on tour, Eleanor records that with the exception of one violent encounter with New York law enforcement, they were everywhere treated with courtesy and respect. And, as Eleanor also notes, even the bourgeoisie had to reckon the tour a success.

The Avelings' success testifies, first, to the talents of the speakers. Eleanor in particular was always remembered as an engaging and fiery lecturer, lucid, funny, and succinct. Aveling, notwithstanding the disrepute in which he is currently held, was admired in labor circles for his dedication and learning, and in learned circles for his fine oratory. The Avelings' American success, however, also attests to the development of the country's labor movement, to what contemporaries called "labor ferment" and to what must have been labor's impressive organizational infrastructure. It is no small thing to turn out a crowd of several hundred workers, let alone workers whose laboring day could be as long as sixteen hours, to audit a speech (Dr. Aveling's) which might last the better part of an hour, then another (Eleanor's) which, though shorter, would inevitably raise a variety of questions about politics and the movement. To contrast the character of the Avelings' tour with either today's major party campaign stumping or minor party invisibility is to get a sense of the conditions under which the lecture tour as political technique can be effective.

The first pages of *The Working-Class Movement in America* are devoted to one of these conditions, namely the existence of an authentic labor press. The papers and journals that the Avelings encounter range from generalist and nationally distributed organs like the famous *John Swinton's Paper* to more narrow and local affairs like New' York's *Furniture Workers' Journal*. Some cities had several labor papers, others had papers in the several languages of their immigrant working populations. Not a few— *The Laborette* of Rawlins or Chicago's *The Women's World*— reflected the degree to which the labor movement had succeeded in reaching and activating the growing population of female wage workers. When the Avelings note that "each journal in the list is a genuine working-class paper, and not, like almost all our English so-called labour prints, a capitalist organ in disguise," they remind us that the literatures of any political bloc do not merely *reflect* given interests and opinion, but are themselves material elements in its formation, serving to shape and link constituencies that would not otherwise exist. Genuine working-class literatures are not just *about* the working class. They are *of* the class, vital to its self-consciousness and practical self-making.

The Working-Class Movement in America makes its own contribution to working-class literature by reworking the bourgeois travelogue. Much as journals project a certain view of the world, one consonant with the class' social and political investments (themselves reproduced in the manufacture, delivery and sale of news and entertainment), so, too, the traveler's report instantiates and integrates class practices and ideologies. Though the Avelings' visit to America precedes the development of capitalist mass tourist industries by more than half a century, the continental Grand Tour and tours of America were already important to the cultivation of European middle-class tastes, institutions and leadership in a period witnessing the transition from mercantilist to imperialist strategies of accumulation. These wandering researches not only contributed to middle-class ideologies and entertainments but very often provided valuable survey information to industrialists and to the state.[26]

Today, of course, tourism is huge global industry; according to some estimates, it is second only to energy and arms. Its growth is central to the dynamics of global development and dependence and, relatedly, to the generation of much of the "knowledge" we have about the peoples of the world. As the need for countertourism becomes more urgent, the organizational and representational significance of the Avelings' American visit becomes more apparent. *The Working-Class Movement in America* is socialist cartography, important as much for how it was made (and with whom it was shared) as for what it describes. Socialist tours and reports develop reliable partisan intelligence while extending interorganizational solidarity. The Avelings' tour taught American workers about the ideas of Karl Marx, but it also gave them information about each other and about struggles "abroad." Much of what Eleanor learned while on tour was to prove invaluable to her own work in London's East End. Aaron Rosebury, a Russian immigrant in London, would take the Avelings' report from that quarter back to America, where for many years he served as an editor, writer, and translator for the Ladies' Garment Workers Union.

In this respect, the Avelings' book develops a tradition that Engels helped to pioneer with his *The Condition of the Working Class in England*. That work, published in 1844, resulted from Engels' first visit to Britain, where he spent some twenty months making industrial excursions from his base in Manchester. Engels' report was held in great esteem by Marx (who had not previously been overimpressed by Engels' intellect); Mehring deemed it "epoch-making" and a "fundamental Socialist work." Lenin had this to say:

> Many descriptions of the dreadful conditions under which the workers live had appeared before Engels came on the scene. And many had urged that something should be done to improve the lot of the proletariat. But Engels was the first to show that the workers were something more than a social class in distress.... He saw that the proletariat would be forced to join the struggle for freedom. Self-help is the motto of militant workers on the march to freedom. Those were the fundamental ideas expressed in Engels' book. Those ideas are now a commonplace among workers who think for themselves.[27]

The Avelings' is a similarly interested document, making no attempt to hide the authors' guiding concern:

> The Working-Class Question is the same in America as in Europe. There, the reiterated, always more pressing inquiry, which is not only the working-class question but *the* social

question of today, is uttered with even more emphasis that in England. The inquiry, variously fashioned and variously formulated, is yet always in essence the same, and for practical purposes may be put into these words: Why is it that the actual producers and distributors of wealth own the least wealth, and those who are not its actual producers and distributors own most wealth?[28]

Why indeed? Visitors to America (and her own cartographers) had long asked the question and had pointed to a variety of factors accounting for the absence of socialism in America—the shallowness of her feudal past, the strength of the country's liberal traditions, the availability of land, the satisfactions (apple pie and so on) of American workers. The most thoughtful of these essays note the intensity and persistence of class struggle in America and invoke such factors to explain the relative weakness of socialism as a working-class ideology. Less scrupulous authors have used working-class political quiescence to demonstrate America's essential social harmony, as if the question were not "why no socialism?" but rather "why no class conflict?" Little embarrassed by the mountains of evidence pointing to long traditions of both capitalist brutality and proletarian struggle, generations of ideologues have surveyed an idealized American terrain and handed in their reports: capitalism in America is freedom itself.[29]

The Avelings departed immediately from the well-beaten exceptionalist path to record the most up-to-date methods of exploitation and to amplify workers' bitter resentments. They describe workers' experimentations in resistance and control and share their assessments of organizational strengths and weaknesses. Most importantly, they "explain the reason why there is, and always must be, a working-class question, until that question is solved by the historic, evolutionary, and revolutionary method, that socialism alone points out as inevitable."[30]

Today we would likely balk at the choice of the word inevitable, even as a cheerleading device. Too much water has passed under the bridge for us to believe that History moves inexorably in the direction of proletarian victory. And yet the thought is not so easily dismissed. In the *Manifesto* (quoted at length in the preface to the 1887 American edition of *Condition*), Marx and Engels indicated the political complexity of revolutionary Marxism when they wrote that "the communists do not form a separate party opposed to other working class parties . . . and have no interests separate and apart from those of the proletariat as a whole."[31] These "communists" distinguish themselves by emphasizing the "common interests of the entire proletariat," by representing the "interests of the movement as a whole." They are, then, both fused with and distinct from particular working-class institutions and campaigns. Historically, this same complexity makes itself felt in a certain temporal perspective: communists "fight for the attainment of immediate ends, for the enforcement of the momentary interests of the working class; but in the movement of the present, they represent and take care of the future of the movement."

These lines reveal why the revolutionary socialist tradition has been at once so fragile and so durable. Fragile, because revolution is no mean achievement—there is nothing preordained about it. Durable, because if actually existing capitalism is war on humanity, then its abolition is the only conceivable human settlement. Between almost impossible and strangely necessary lies, of course, the terrain of socialist history, the terrain of the struggle itself.

In the "state of the struggle" portion of their report, the Avelings give cause for both hope and alarm. As is well known, the Avelings were not in perfect political sympathy with their sponsors. In Engels' writings, the word "sect" often appears in conjunction with the Socialist Labor Party; he was of the opinion that this German-American and largely New York-based group had become something apart from the working class. It had remade Marxism into an ossified and pedantic dogmatics, in which form it would not only fail in revolutionary effect but would cease to be intelligible. The Avelings did spend much of their time carrying on the SLP's polemic against anarchism, but they understood the appeal of Parson's "Chicago Idea" (if not Most's adventurism), and they joined the movement to defend the Haymarket martyrs.[32] But Eleanor was sharply critical of her socialist hosts' "principled" unwillingness to learn and work in English, their unwonted arrogance, and their distance from the main thoroughfares of working-class life.[33]

Eleanor, however, saw sectarian dispute as premature in the American context and addressed herself to "unconscious socialists"—men and women who were fully acquainted with capitalism's cruelties and irrationalities but who were in need of basic political and theoretical orientation. Her stock speech sought to disabuse her audiences of their misprisions about socialism: socialists will not, she argued, deprive people of their private property, if by private property we mean personal belongings. To the contrary, it is capitalism that ensures that only the few have such property, and it is only through the socialization of real and productive property that "property rights" becomes meaningful for the millions who have never known economic security and freedom from want.

She assessed the achievements of working-class formations in relation to such socialist basics. The Knights of Labor, whose phenomenal growth in the year of the tour was matched by phenomenal shrinkage in the years to follow, naturally impressed the Avelings, who did not miss the meaning of the Knights' success: here were millions of American workers—native born and immigrant, skilled and unskilled, men and women—demanding not only shorter hours and better wages but political and industrial power. But they foresaw difficulties. The Knights were top-heavy with "labor aristocrats" and the Order's leadership was ideologically conservative, often emphasizing community over class, cooperation over revolution. Grand Master Workman John Powderly's vacillations on the necessity of strikes and political activity indicated ominous misalignments. Between the rank and file and the leadership a threatening faultline was already visible. Between the working class and the bourgeoisie the chasm had not been widened enough. Historians find different ways to mark the beginning of the Order's end, but for some—those who point to the second Gould strike, to Powderly's groveling visit to the Holy See, or to the shocking conduct of District Assembly 49 during the Cigar Makers' Union's lockout—the death knell had been sounded by 1886.[34] Correctly, the Avelings predicted a split in the offing.

The Avelings were most excited by the emergence of independent proletarian political parties. New York's United Labor Party (from which both Gompers and Powderly remained aloof) conducted a stunning mayoral campaign involving most of the existing New York unions and witnessing the elaboration of several innovative political techniques. The United Labor Party established its own naturalization bureau, which quickly made citizens of thousands of Henry George supporters. A variety of labor councils, necessary to coordinate unions and to advance political cohesion, were established. George's candidacy in 1886 was supported by out-of-state unions and workers; at least one Canadian assembly of the Knights made a campaign contribution.

Outside of New York, labor candidates were run for hundreds of national, state, and municipal posts. Where these campaigns failed to capture office, they made respectable showings; in the wake of Haymarket, the United Labor Party in Chicago captured 25 percent of the vote. Engels, back in England, recorded the impression that the movement made on foreigners: "In Europe the effect of the American elections in November was tremendous. The very fact that the movement is so sharply accentuated as a labor movement and has sprung up so suddenly and forcefully has stunned the people completely."[35]

The movement stunned the capitalists as well, and in the wake of the 1886 agitations, the counteroffensive began in earnest. Employers responded violently to the shock of May Day. Lockouts, "iron-clad" agreements, Pinkertons, and blacklisting were the favored industrial tactics. Capital's allies in the repressive apparatuses invented new legal weapons (most significantly, the court-ordered injunction); a rash of conspiracy charges and the Haymarket executions began the state's march to Pullman (1894), which would witness the army deployed against striking workers. The established political parties, forced to contend with labor's electoral upsurge, set to bribing and infiltrating. Like company unions, their ersatz Labor Clubs steered working-class ideas and energy safely into bourgeois harbors. In the meantime, middle-class rightward drift was affecting the genuine labor parties. George turned tail within a year; the expulsion of the socialists by his worthy henchmen inaugurated a series of disruptions, splits, and stumblings, which by 1888 had eviscerated the movement for independent political action. Of the movements of 1886, only the quietly founded AFL had any significant institutional future.[36]

⚒ ⚒ ⚒

Looking to the future of the movement as a whole, socialists have maintained an abiding interest in the events of 1886, for they serve to remind us that when working people organize to advance their interests, humanity takes a step forward. *The Working-Class Movement in America* is both a monument to and a part of this rich if discontinuous history-in-the-making. The men and women of 1886—the Avelings amongst them—met one another on new terrain, and they explored it with uncommon courage and intelligence. They learned, invented, smashed, and built, remaking bits of the world to suit a common humanity. In the process, they themselves became more human. And they knew it, for they had claimed it.

For Eleanor Marx, socialism was just this bumpy and interrupted history of a free humanity. As translator, courier, lecturer, and writer she worked to forge links between history's humans, between their dead pasts—which found them separated by conditions not of their choosing—and their collective and living future. Returning from another of her tours (through Scotland, where, unsurprisingly, she delivered a lecture called "The Working-Class Movement Abroad"), she wrote to her sponsors at the Aberdeen Socialist Society:

> Dear Comrades,
> I am back again in our murky London, but even our London fog seems quite bright and pleasant when I think of the happy time I spent with you in Aberdeen. It was such a delight—and help—to find people *alive*—as you are, when most of us are so dead—and eager and hardworking for the Cause. Assuredly whenever I feel despondent (and there are times when one can't

help desponding) I shall think of Aberdeen and take heart again.[37]

For Eleanor Marx, life began and ended with the struggle. I believe this is how she would choose to be remembered.

NOTES

1. Marx's eldest daughter, Jenny, died shortly before Marx himself. Laura, living in France, and in any case less politically involved, often accepted the role of translator, correspondent, and tactical advisor. But it was Eleanor who inherited Marx's political passion and single-mindedness and who devoted her life to the work.

2. "Mohr" was a common nickname of Eleanor's father, whose dark complexion—some said—gave him the appearance of a Moor. A surprising amount of Eleanor's correspondence is devoted to the design and upkeep of Marx's grave, and much of her writing is dedicated to answering his detractors—Bismarck amongst them—whose slanders were postponed until the target was unable to defend himself. Eleanor of course edited a number of Marx's addresses and articles for publication and did the (uncredited) "devil's work" of tracking down his sources in the British Museum. Perhaps the hardest task she inherited ("writing it was worse than having a tooth out!") took the form of introducing Marx's now famous letter to his father. "Ein Brief des jungen Marx" first appeared in *Neue Zeit*, 1897.

3. Amongst the many public anniversaries Eleanor organized was the yearly remembrance of the Paris Commune, where she always spoke with passion of the "eternal life gained by those who fought and fell in the great cause of uplifting humanity." Henry Hyndman, *Record of an Adventurous Life* (London: Macmillan, 1911), p. 346. The funeral of Alfred Linnell, killed by police in an Anti-Coercion demonstration, Eleanor declared "*very* fine, and a great success. The streets were a won-

derful sight. . . . If only the Radicals were not so many of them cowards we would carry the Square." Eleanor Marx to Laura Lafargue, December 31, 1887, in Olga Meier, Faith Evans, and Sheila Rowbotham, *The Daughters of Karl Marx: Family Correspondence, 1866–1898* (New York: Harcourt Brace Jovanovich 1982), pp. 202–203.

4. See, for example, her article "Evil May Day," which appeared in the *Weekly Times and Echo* on May 6, 1894. In 1517, the artisans of London had attacked resident foreigners upon whom they blamed their declining position. Eleanor's article drew parallels with the May Day celebrations of the late nineteenth century and reminded readers of the dangers of xenophobic prejudice. She must have relished the task of challenging Lujo Brentano, an old paternal critic, on his history of the English guilds (*Neue Zeit*, "Wie Lujo Brentano zitiert," 1894).

5. Coauthored with Edward Aveling, the essay was first published in 1886 in the *Westminster Review*. It is now available through International Publishers (New York: 1987), under the title *Thoughts on Women and Society*. "Most women suicides are between the ages of sixteen and twenty-one. Many of these, of course, are due to the pregnancy which our social system drags down to the level of a crime. But others are due to ungratified sex instincts, often concealed under the euphemism 'disappointed love.' . . . As with all crimes, the criminal is not the individual sufferer but the society that forces her to sin and suffer."

6. Yvonne Kapp's definitive and engaging two volume biography of Eleanor Marx provides the necessary and meticulously researched factual record against which these narratives may be judged. Published in the United States by Pantheon in 1972, *Eleanor Marx* is now out of print.

7. Lewis S. Feuer, *Marx and the Intellectuals: A Set of Post-Ideological Essays* (New York: Anchor, 1969) p. 141ff.

8. Feuer's distortions of the historical record (to leave aside his distortions of Marxist theory) are too numerous to delineate. But his wholly uncritical reliance upon the testimony of Hyndman—a proven and life-long libeler when it came to the Marx family—is fair indication of his method and scruples.

9. Robert Banner's avenging letter in the *Labor Leader* (April, 1898) set the tone for these narratives and established the "record" upon which later accounts rely. It is again Yvonne Kapp who has troubled to investigate Banner's charges. They are quite fantastic and were only further embellished by Bernstein: "Was Eleanor Marx in den Tod trieb?" *Neue Zeit*, 1898, and *My Years in Exile* (London: L. Parsons, 1921); Hardie, *Labor Leader*, July 30, 1898; and Hyndman, op. cit. C. Tsuzuki's account of Eleanor's death in *The Life of Eleanor Marx: A Socialist Tragedy* (Oxford: Clarendon, 1967) relies entirely upon Banner's "documentary" evidence, as does R. Florence's *Marx's Daughters* (New York: The Dial Press, 1975).

10. With Samuel Moore, Aveling produced the first English translation of *Capital*, under Engels' supervision. A quick glance at his political and publishing record reveals both dedication and consistency in orientation.

11. Two such charges were made, one involving the monies of the Social Democratic Federation and a second concerning tour expenses while in America. In each case Aveling responded convincingly enough to satisfy at least Engels, who appears to have genuinely believed that the allegations amounted to sectarian machination. The Gasworkers' Union placed enough trust in Aveling's fiduciary honor to make him an Auditor, and in this role he seems to have acquitted himself admirably.

12. See, for instance, Aaron Rosebury, "Eleanor, Daughter of Marx," *Monthly Review* 24, no. 8 (1973). It is the alleged evaporation of Engels' legacy which stirs most excitement at the Eleanor inquests. In 1895, Engels left to each of Marx's surviving daughters something on the order of 5,000 pounds. Eleanor used her share of the inheritance to buy a house, to set up a trust for Jenny's children, to cover Aveling's extensive medical bills and rest cures and, of course, to supplement her own meager earnings. At the time of her death, she bequeathed Aveling an estate worth about 1,800 pounds. Compared to the Marxes, who went through Karl's 1,500 pound inheritance (the combined legacies of his mother and Wilhelm Wolff) in less than a year, the Avelings seem positively thrifty.

13. Kapp speculates that this fact likely attests to Aveling's sterility. She also believes that Eleanor, who like Aveling's mistresses bore no children, had wanted them. *This* hypothetical "failing" on Aveling's part, more genuinely rare and individual than any disregard for the feelings of a wife, is left unimagined or delicately unmentioned by most who held and hold Aveling responsible for Eleanor's unhappiness. *Eleanor Marx*, vol. 2, p. 76.

14. A materialist account of Eleanor's predicament should center on the question of power: what were the conditions of Aveling's possibility and the conditions of Eleanor's despair? Not until the Russian revolution would the political economy of love and duty begin to be addressed in a systematic and practical way, through the efforts of organized revolutionary women.

15. Kapp, *Eleanor Marx*, vol. 1, p. 21.

16. Engels' choices involved not only political calculations concerning, say, Bernstein's tendency to vacillate on crucial doctrinal matters, or Liebknecht's sheer clumsiness as an organizer and tactician, but also the consideration of more quotidian and practical matters, such as training any heir in Marx's idiosyncratic shorthands and codes. These, of course, were better known to Eleanor than any of those Engels considered.

17. Engels often disagreed with his colleagues' judgments and his correspondence is full of brisk if generally polite criticism of their work. He was genuinely and personally infuriated, however, by the Bernstein-Kautsky-Mehring-Lafargue decision to undertake a multivolume history of socialism without soliciting his contributions. "Of all those alive today, there was only one whose collaboration appeared absolutely necessary and that one was I. I dare go so far as to say that without my help a work of this nature cannot be anything but incomplete and inadequate. Of all possibly useful people I am precisely the only one who was *not* invited to collaborate." Engels to Kautsky, May 1895. The first two statements are indisputable (though, as it happens, the quadrumvirate only failed to contact Engels because, his death quickly and evidently

approaching, they wanted not to burden him with the anxiety of still more work left incomplete). The last gives an indication of Eleanor's standing with the men of the movement.

18. Here is Engels' description, from the 1892 preface to the English re-edition of *The Condition of the Working Class in England*, trans. W. O. Henderson and W. H. Chaloner (New York: Macmillan, 1958), by which the importance of these links to socialism—and thus Eleanor's links to the new unionists—may be gauged: "the 'New Unionism,' that is to say, the organization of the great mass of 'unskilled' workers. This organization may to a great extent adopt the form of the old Unions of 'skilled' workers but it is essentially different in character. The old Unions preserve the traditions of the time when they were founded, and look upon the wages system as a once-for-all established, final fact, which they at best can modify in the interest of their members. The new Unions were founded at a time when the faith in the eternity of the wages system was severely shaken; their founders and promoters were Socialists either consciously or by feeling."

19. Marx misdiagnosed Eleanor's periodic spells of despair and panics that left her insomniac, anorectic, and irritable as attacks of virginity, which condition he deliberately prolonged, and about which he quite unkindly corresponds with Engels.

20. As a socialist, Eleanor knew that so long as wage differentials between women and men were permitted to exist, one half of the class could be played off against another in any industrial or political dispute. And as a feminist, she had no patience with the argument, which working-class men sometimes spared employers the trouble of making, that if women's wages rose, they would cease to be employed at all.

21. Reporting, for instance, Eleanor's 1893 address to an audience of female suffragists, *Justice* (the organ of the Social Democratic Federation, a society that Eleanor joined, split to form the Socialist League, and then, following the League's infiltration by anarchists, rejoined) marked the distinction she made between female suffrage and adult suffrage, commenting, "Fine-lady suffragists of the Mrs. Henry Fawcett

type are quite of the opinion that the poor should keep their place, and if common women as well as common men were to get votes, there's no knowing what use they might make of them."

22. Eleanor, whose youthful political enthusiasm for the Fenians was encouraged by Engels' companion Lizzie Burns, toured the country with the pair in 1869. She would often recall her visit and her father's analysis of the Irish question, recorded for posterity in the famous letter to Kugelmann: "The English working class can never do anything decisive here in England until it separates its policy towards Ireland in the most definite way from the policy of the ruling classes ... not as a matter of sympathy with Ireland but as a demand made in the interests of the English proletariat." At the Brussels Conference, Eleanor's *Report from Great Britain and Ireland,* later published as a penny pamphlet, made reference to an address she herself had given at a demonstration before members of the Gasworkers' Union, whose Irish membership numbered in the tens of thousands. She was especially pleased to report that "no words were more enthusiastically cheered ... than 'Let Ireland be free, but let it be an Ireland of free workers; it matters little to the men and women of Ireland if they are exploited by Nationalists or Orangemen.'"

23. Two examples: first, Christmas, 1884, in the wake of the Socialist League's split from the SDF: "[Hyndman's] aim has been to make the movement seem big; to frighten the powers that be with a turnip bogie which perhaps he almost believes in himself: hence all that insane talk about immediate forcible revolution, when we know that the workers in England are not even touched by the movement." Second, November 16, 1887, in the wake of Bloody Sunday: "I hear that our fire-eating anarchists here as usual are getting frightened now that there is a little danger and that Morris on Monday declared a demonstration useless, and that the revolution won't be made until the people are armed. He doesn't seem capable of understanding that by the time the people are armed, there will be no need for the Revolution (with a very big 'R')."

24. The 1886 delegation from the Continent did include Liebknecht, who arrived a bit behind the Avelings and returned to Europe a few weeks ahead of them. Liebknecht's account of his American visit, *Ein Blick in die neue Welt* (Stuttgart: J. H. W. Dietz, 1887), had nothing to say either about the U.S. working class or the possibilities for socialism in America. Indeed, Liebknecht argued that the "great transatlantic republic" was exactly an exceptional political economy, governed by forces and powers quite distinct from those at work in Europe. Kautsky's review of the book showed clear signs of embarrassment and it is interesting to note the power of exceptionalist ideologies over even the most committed and informed of socialists.

25. Legally, of course, Eleanor was not Aveling's wife. Indeed, at the time Eleanor issued her "marriage" announcements, Aveling had been married to Isabel Campbell Frank for over a decade. That Eleanor produced and held to her matrimonial fiction tends to be understood as an effort not to offend the tender sensibilities of nineteenth-century prudes. In fact, Eleanor was always candid about and unembarrassed by her domestic situation and certainly women of her generation were well acquainted with the practice of cohabitation. Mrs. Marx-Aveling needed no sexual cover. She needed a new situation and a new passport into socialist circles. She needed to bury the "minx." This is what Aveling gave her, and it is, paradoxically, only as Mrs. Marx-Aveling that Eleanor comes into her own.

26. An interesting examination of the role of travel literatures in the development of capitalism is provided by Mary Louise Pratt, *Imperial Eyes: Travel Writing and Transculturation* (New York: Routledge, 1992). The Avelings were acutely aware of the traveler's place in the reproduction of class hierarchies. Eleanor's first impressions of America, recorded in her correspondence with Laura and in an article for the *New Yorker Volkszeitung* concern the "rudeness and brutality of the so-called better classes" in whose company she crossed the Atlantic. Notable for their ability to "laughingly look at the poor emigrants lying on the deck in their wretched clothes without the least sign of sym-

pathy," these traveling Americans disgusted Aveling as well. See his *An American Journey* (New York, John W. Lovell Company, 1887).

27. Engels, *The Condition of the Working Class in England*, pp. xii–xiii.

28. *The Working-Class Movement in America*, p. 69 in this volume.

29. Amongst intellectuals, Hartz, Huntington, Sombart, and Tocqueville remain the idealists of choice. Fukuyama's recent variation on the theme was perhaps less academically respectable, but each generation must rewrite its myths anew, and Fukuyama's seems to have captured the post-Soviet market.

30. *The Working-Class Movement*, p. 69 in this volume.

31. Marx and Engels, writing well before the historical development of social democratic parties and still farther in advance of the Russian Revolution, used the word "communist" to refer narrowly to members of the Communist League (1847–1852) and more generally to anyone sharing their perspective.

32. Albert Parsons was active in a mass working-class current that blended anarchist hostility to the state with a more Marxist organizational orientation, the latter far less visible in the "pure" anarchism of Johann Most, whose favored tactics remained the *attentat* and incendiary rhetoric. Back in England the Avelings joined the international movement to free the Chicago Eight.

33. See Philip S. Foner, *History of the Labor Movement in the United States*, vol. 2 (New York: International Publishers, 1955), pp. 42ff.

34. On the Knights, see Foner, op. cit., pp. 157ff. Also Leon Fink, *Workingmen's Democracy* (Urbana: University of Illinois Press, 1983), and Kim Voss, *The Making of American Exceptionalism: The Knights of Labor and Class Formation in the Nineteenth Century* (Ithaca, N.Y.: Cornell University Press, 1995).

35. Engels to Sorge, November 1886, in *Letters to Americans* (New York: International Publishers, 1953).

36. It would be inaccurate to say that after 1886 all independent

labor politics in the United States ceased. Labor councils, the eight-hour movement, and a variety of democratic-trade union alliances struggled along. But there was a definite decline. As Kim Moody notes in his essay in this volume, things were *not* much the same in 1891 and the Homestead strike of 1892 marked a definite watershed.

37. Eleanor to William Diack, January 27, 1893 in Kapp, p. 539. Emphasis in the original.

The Working-Class Movement in America
by Edward and Eleanor Marx Aveling

1 | Introduction

The Working-Class Question is the same in America as in Europe. There the reiterated, always more pressing inquiry, which is not only the working-class question but *the* social question today, is uttered with even more reiteration and emphasis than in England. The inquiry, variously fashioned and variously formulated, is yet always in essence the same, and for practical purposes may be put in these words: Why is it that the actual producers and distributors of wealth own least wealth, and those who are not its actual producers and distributors own most wealth?

It would be foolish, and more, on our part, to deny that the phrase "Working-Class Question in America" is to us in the main synonymous with the phrase "Socialism in America." We believe that Socialism explains the reason why there is, and always must be, a "working-class question," until that question is solved by the historic, evolutionary, and revolutionary method, that Socialism alone points out as inevitable. But whilst this is the case with the beginning of the real working-class movement in any country—and it really has begun in America—there must be mixed up with that beginning so much of confusion, of false starts, of marching and countermarching, of apparent conflict between those that actually have the same end at heart, and of very real conflict between the slowly awakening masses, on the one hand and the many blind led by the wittingly or unwittingly blind, on the other that, in a sense, any account of the working-class question has to do with certain elements that are other than socialistic.

And, first, a few words on our credentials to deal with the subject. These consist of some study of the questions under discussion in this country [Britain], observation of the great proletarian movement in Europe and America through the medium of the labor press of other lands, a fifteen weeks' tour through America under the auspices of the Socialist Labor Party. The second and third of these alone call for a moment's notice.

The ordinary reader has little or no idea of the amount of purely working-class journalism that there is abroad. Here we cannot pause to say anything upon the English newspapers that are really devoted to the cause of labor. But we may ask the reader not to form his estimate of the magnitude of the working-class movement from the meager list of journals of this kind to be found in England. In every other of the chief European countries the journalistic strength of the proletarian movement, where oppression by the authorities has not been resorted to, is much greater than in this. But in connection with the special object before us the following list of some of the chief working-class papers of the United States is of interest:

Labor Journal, Alpena, Mich.; *The Talk*, Anna, Ill.; *The Trades' Union*, Atchison, Kans.; *People's Advocate*, Atlantic, Cass Co., Iowa; *The Free Press*, Baltimore, Mich.; *The Labor Vindicator*, Bay City, Mich.; *The Labor Leader*, Boston, Mass.; *The Missouri*

Industry, Brookfield, Mo.; *The Agitator*, Bridgeport, Conn.; *Morning Justice*, Burlington, Iowa; *The Signal*, Champaign, Ill.; *The Carpenter*, Cleveland, Ohio; *The Chicago Express*, Chicago, Ill.; *Arbeiter Zeitung*, Chicago, Ill.; *The Sentinel*, Chicago, Ill.; *The Unionist*, Cincinnati, Ohio; *Cloud Country Critic*, Condordia, Kans.; *Iowa Plain Dealer*, Cresco, Iowa; *The Commonwealth*, Creston, Iowa; *The Dayton Workman*, Dayton, Ohio; *Daily Labor Bulletin*, Decatur, Ill.; *The Labor Leaf*, Detroit, Mich.; *The Labor Enquirer*, Denver, Colo.; *Workman*, Durham, N.C.; *Easton Labor Journal*, Easton, Pa.; *Anti-Monopolist Enterprise*, Dickinson Co., Kans.; *Western Watchman*, Eureka, Humboldt Co., Calif.; *The Weekly Protest*, Exeter, N.H.; *Labor Advocate*, Galveston, Tex.; *The Signal*, Grinnell, Iowa; *The Palladium*, Hamilton, Ont.; *American Liberty*, Hampton, Va.; *The Laborer*, Haverhill, Mass.; *Labor Echo*, Houston, Tex.; *Industrial Record*, Jacksonville, Fla.; *Joliet Weekly News*, Joliet, Ill.; *Labor Organizer*, Kansas City, Mo.; *The Equator*, Key West, Fla.; *El Jornalero*, Key West, Fla.; *Labor Advocate*, Lewiston, Maine; *The Radical*, Litchfield, Minn.; *Saturday Evening Union*, Los Angeles, Calif.; *The Labor Record*, Louisville, Ky.; *The Knight of Labor*, Lynn, Mass.; *Budget*, Manchester, N.H.; *Menominee River Laborer*, Marinette, Men. Co., Mich.; *Die Tribune*, Indianapolis, Ind.; *The Weekly Record*, Memphis, Tenn.; *Arbeiter Zeitung*, Milwaukee, Wis.; *Labor Review*, Milwaukee, Wis.; *Free Press*, Millersville, Pa.; *Rights of Man*, Mount Vernon, Ind.; *The Liberal*, Nashville, Tenn.; *The Agitator*, Nangatnek, Conn.; *Workman's Advocate*, New Haven, Conn.; *New Jersey Unionist*, Newark, N.J.; *The People*, Providence, N.Y.; *Backer Zeitung, Boycotter, Der Sozialist, Furniture Workers' Journal, Irish World, John Swinton's Paper, Our Country, Progress, Leader, Volks Zeitung, Standard*, all of New York City; *The Sentinel*, Norwich, N.Y.; *Progress*, Omaha, Nebr.; *The State*

Standard, Parkersville, West Va.; *Labor Standard*, Paterson, N.J.; *The Voice of Labor*, Petersburg, Ill.; *National Labor Tribune*, Pittsburgh, Pa.; *The Labor Herald*, Pittsburgh, Pa.; *Granite Cutters' Journal, Tageblatt*, Philadelphia, Pa.; *The Avant Courier*, Portland, Ore.; *Kansas Workman*, Anenema, Kans.; *The Laborette*, Rawlins; *Labor Herald*, Richmond, Va.; *The Capital*, Richmond, Va.; *The Southern Artizan*, Richmond, Va.; *Anti-Monopolist*, Wentworth Block, Rochester, N.H.; *The Rockland Opinion*, Rockland, Maine; *Rock Islander*, Rock Island, Ill.; *The Champion*, St. Louis, Mo.; *The Oregon Vidette*, Salem, Oregon; *Die Tribune* and *Puget Sound Weekly Co-operator*, Seattle, Wash.; *The Labor Union*, Sedalia, Mo.; *The Sheboygan*, Sheboygan Falls, Wis.; *The Voice of Labor*, Springfield, Ill.; *The Mail*, Eldridge Building, Stockton, Calif.; *The Laborer*, Syracuse, N.Y.; *The Industrial News*, Toledo, Ohio.

It should be noted (1) that this is not a complete list, especially as regards the large number of German papers that are published weekly or daily, and are avowedly proletarian in character; (2) that probably each journal in the list is a genuine working-class paper, and not, like almost all our English so-called labor prints, a capitalist organ in disguise.

Dealing, however briefly, with our recent tour through the States, involved a certain amount of personal reference only justifiable by the desire to show that we have had exceptional opportunities for observation during our stay in America. From September 10 to October 1 New York was our center. During these three weeks large audiences were addressed in New York, its suburbs, and neighboring towns to the number of some half-dozen. On October 2 we left New York on a twelve weeks' tour, visiting in all some thirty-five places. This tour included the New England towns, the Lake towns, the West as far as Kansas City, whence we worked steadily back to New York.

In all these places at least one meeting was held, and in some places as many as four meetings. These were, with the very rarest exceptions, largely attended. In many places hundreds of people were unable to gain admission. The audiences were, without any exception at all, most attentive. We have never spoken to any audiences like the American for patience, fairness, anxiety to get at the meaning of the speaker. To say that all, or even the majority of the listeners agreed with the views laid before them, would be inaccurate. But to say that all gave a fair hearing, and that the majority at least understood what was meant, is to say the truth.

The fact is the American people were waiting to hear in their own language what Socialism was. Until this time its doctrines had been consciously and deliberately preached, as a rule, only by Germans. Of systematic and general declaration of them in the English tongue there had been practically nothing. This is the real significance of the tour of 1886. For the first time the American public were brought clearly face to face with the principles of a teaching they had ridiculed and condemned without understanding.

That this is the case was shown by the tone of the press. [Wilhelm] Liebknecht,* our German friend and coworker, and ourselves were, on our arrival in America, assailed with all the violence, virulence, and misrepresentation of which portions of the press in that country are capable. Our meetings, if reported at all, were dismissed in a few lines of inaccurate statement. Within

---

*For writings, speeches, and biographical material of this outstanding leader of the German socialist movement, including information on his U.S. tour, see William A. Pelz, ed., *Wilhelm Liebknecht and German Social Democracy: A Documentary History* (Westport, Conn.: Greenwood Press, 1994), an invaluable resource.

three weeks all this was changed, and from that time to the end of the tour every leading newspaper in every town, from New York to Rockville, gave full and fair accounts of interviews, of the meetings, and of the speeches. Thus, for some three months the American public had in town after town from one to three or four columns in each of the leading papers wholly given over to socialistic teaching, to say nothing of the countless leaders devoted to the demolition and advertisement of our doctrines.

And in every town we met, both in private and in public, the leading men and women in the various working-class organizations. Most of our days were spent in the presence of, and conversation with, the rank and file as well as the leaders of those organizations. Our position in respect to them was that of learners rather than of teachers. We were anxious to gather from them all the facts and generalizations possible. Some of these facts and generalizations, together with certain of our own observations, we now lay before the reader.

2 | General Impressions

The first general impression left on the mind is, that in this country of extremes, those of poverty and wealth, of exploitation in its active and passive form, are more marked than in Europe. In America transition stages and classes are, for the most part, wanting. The extremes of temperature in one place, and the suddenness of the passage from one extreme to another, are quite unparalleled in England. Again, in America there seems to be no social and intellectual middle class. The cultured American is perhaps the most charming person on the face of the earth. The manners and customs of the average American, on the other hand, are, for the most part, indescribably unpleasant. Between these two there appear to be no mean. The middle-class set of people that make up the majority of the English folk with whom we come into contact—that large number of quite ordinary but very pleasant, well-bred, decently read English people, with whom you can comfortably spend an evening, if you would not care to spend a life—are apparently almost unrepresented in America. It must be understood that in our strictures on the manners of the average American we are not dealing with the working classes. We were everywhere struck with the excessive kindliness and courtesy of the working men and women of America. In all places we found that these, whether they were officials like the tram conductors or our fellow-travellers, in street or by car, set an example of good breeding that the American moneyed man and woman might do well to follow.

So it is also in class relations. There are in America far more trenchant distinctions between the capitalist and laboring class than in the older lands. This distinction is not, as in the latter, bridged over and refined down by many examples of intermediate classes. It stands out clearly and uncompromisingly. At the one end of the scale is the millionaire, openly, remorselessly crushing out all rivals, swallowing up all the feebler folk. At the other end is the helpless, starving proletarian. Towards this last the multitude of the people are gravitating thither. The real division of society into two classes, the laborer and the capitalist, veiled in England and other European countries by the remains of old systems, by artificial classes of royalty, nobility, and so forth, in America stares one in the face. No such remnants of old systems, no surviving classes that belonged to these, exist in America. The capitalist system came here as a ready-made article, and with all the force of its inherent, uncompromising brutality, it thrust on the notice of every one the fact that in society today there are only two classes, and that these are enemies.

With the more clear demarcation of these two classes, each the necessary complement of the other, there is also the more clear recognition of their antagonism. In England, to a large extent, the attempt to make the workers believe that there is a community of interests between them and their employers still succeeds. Not only do the employers make the men and women they own believe this; they actually persuade themselves to some extent that it is true. But in America this mutual deception is nearly at an end. The working men and the capitalists in the majority of cases quite understand that each, as a class, is the deadly and inexorable foe of the other; that no ultimate *modus vivendi* is possible between them; that the next years of the nineteenth century will be taken up chiefly by an internecine struggle, that will end, as the capitalists hope, in the subjugation of the working class; as the working men know, in the abolition of all classes.

The second general impression to be noted is this; that the condition of the working class is no better in America than in England. To this very important conclusion we have not so much come as we have been driven. We believe it to be absolutely irrefutable. The conclusion rests on four main bases: (1) the evidence furnished by the daily press of America; (2) our own observations during fifteen weeks; (3) the evidence given by the hundreds of working men and women—Germans, English, Irish, and Americans—of whom we made careful and detailed inquiries; (4) statistics furnished by the Bureau of Labor Reports.

All four classes of evidence point to the same conclusion. Setting aside, in both countries, hardship or of notably high wage, and taking the average condition of the average wage-laborer in the two countries, his condition in the one is, to all intents and purposes, precisely as bad as it is in the other. In the present chapter we do not propose to give any of the evidence on which this generalization rests. But in its successors we propose to deal at length with two classes only of that evidence. Certain details that came under our own personal observation will be given, and the statistics from the reports furnished by the Bureaus of Labor for the different States will be quoted at length. These last yield infinitely the most valuable results, for two reasons. First, they cover wide areas and numberless cases; second, they are official documents, unbiased by any sentiment in favor of labor.

And here we are tempted to ask, "Where are the American writers of fiction?" With a subject, and such a subject, lying ready to their very hands, clamoring at their very doors, not one of them touches it.* Even in England, where we have no novelist belonging to the school of Henry James or W. D. Howells, some sort of attempt at dealing with the relative position of rich and poor, and even with their relative antagonism, has here and there been made. Charles Dickens, Walter Besant, Disraeli in *The Two Nations*, whether they understood the real nature of the questions at issue or not, at least touched on them. But of the American novelists none of repute has pictured for us the New York or Boston proletariat. From a double point of view this seems strange. The American is nothing if not descriptive, photographic; and the society in the midst of which he lives cries aloud to be pictured by him. We have portraits of "ladies," of Daisy Millers, and so forth. But there are no studies of factory-hands and of dwellers in tenement houses; no pictures of those sunk in the innermost depths of the modern Inferno. Yet these types will be, must be, dealt with; and one of these days the *Uncle Tom's Cabin* of Capitalism will be written.

The third general impression is the prevalence of what we call unconscious Socialism. This unconscious sentiment is less preva-

---

*This literary comment has obvious validity yet is overstated. Within two decades a proliferating number of important U.S. writers were to deal with working-class experience, but even before the 1880s this experience had been reflected in the poetry of Walt Whitman, as well as in Herman Melville's novel *Moby Dick*, not to mention Rebecca Harding Davis's minor classic *Life in the Iron Mills*, among other works. See relevant commentary in such diverse sources as C. L. R. James, *American Civilization* (Cambridge, Mass.: Blackwell, 1993), pp. 50–85, Granville Hicks, *The Great Tradition* (New York: Macmillan, 1933), pp. 20–31, and Walter B. Rideout, *The Radical Novel in the United States, 1900–1954* (Cambridge: Harvard University Press, 1956), pp. 1–18.

lent in England than in America, simply because in the former country there has been of late years more clear and distinct preaching of the doctrines of Socialism, by voice and book, than in the latter. Within the last few years, in England, a considerable number of sentimental Socialists have been forthcoming. By sentimental Socialists we mean men and women who felt that things were wrong, and felt that they ought to be righted. These, coming across the teaching of Socialism, which show why things are wrong, and how they are to be righted, have, without understanding these teachings, except imperfectly, yet felt their accuracy, felt that they offer at once the only explanation of the present, and the only solution of the future. Now, in England a large number of people feeling thus have declared themselves Socialists, and their Socialism is, even if it be a little helpless, no longer unconscious.

But in America the opportunity that these have had and embraced, has not until recently been forthcoming.* The popular idea of Socialism was everywhere there, as it is still to a large extent in England, one of misconception founded on misrepresentation. The placing of Socialism and its principles before the people has, however, been followed in America, as in England, by the discovery of a vast amount of this unconscious Socialism. Large numbers of persons, finding at last that Socialism does not mean equal division of property, nor the application of dynamite to capitalists, nor anarchy, have in town after town, by hundred upon hundred, declared, "Well, if that is Socialism we are Socialists."

It must not be, for one moment, imagined from this that the

---

*The first book-length English-language exposition of Marxist-influenced socialism published in the United States is probably Laurence Gronlund's 1884 work *The Cooperative Commonwealth*, edited with an introduction by Stow Persons (Cambridge: Harvard University Press, 1965), which—along with the present volume—is one of the most valuable and informative critiques of U.S. capitalism from this period.

doctrines preached by us, as the mouthpieces for the time being of the Socialist party, were not revolutionary. These were, as all Socialist teaching must be, of the most revolutionary character. The mistake into which the Americans had fallen was the common one, that Anarchism is revolutionary. Anarchism is reactionary, and the Socialist Labor Party of America, like its most recent speakers, are not Anarchists because they are revolutionists.

Still more important than even the adhesion by word of mouth and in many cases by membership of so many unconscious Socialists of the sentimental type, was the significant discovery of the vast body of unconscious working-class Socialists. With these again it was the same story, but with a sequel the full meaning of which can be grasped only by those who know that the Socialist movement can never be a real one in any country until it is a working-class movement. The mass of the American working class had scarcely any more conception of the meaning of Socialism than had "their betters." They also had been grievously misled by capitalist papers and capitalist economists and preachers. Hence it came to pass that after most of our meetings we were met by Knights of Labor, Central Labor Union men, and members of other working-class organizations, who told us that they, entering the place antagonists to Socialism as they fancied, had discovered that for a long time past they had been holding its ideas. Upon this, by far the most significant aspect of the widely spread unconscious Socialism, we shall have more to say when we consider the working-class organizations in detail.

With the economic condition of the working class in America, with the chief working-class organizations, with the recent political movement, and with the leaders of that movement, we shall deal in the chapters that follow.

3 | The General Condition of American Workers

The average condition of the average wage-laborer in America is as bad as it is in England.* In support of this, our chief evidence will be taken from the latest annual reports of the Bureau of Labor for the various States. For these reports, together with much valuable oral information, we are indebted to Colonel Carroll D. Wright, the head of the Massachusetts Bureau (the first established in America), from the time of its founding until now. Colonel Wright is also the head of the Central Bureau, established in 1884, at Washington. The work of this central office is the generalizing the generalizations of the individual States, for the benefit of the Union as a whole.

Here is a list of the States in which these Bureaux are at work, with the date of the founding of each: Massachusetts, 1869; Penn-

---

*While we have noted in the introduction—citing Frederick Engels—that developments in U.S. industry facilitated rising living standards within the working class, there is also considerable data to back up this assertion by Marx and Aveling regarding U.S. and British conditions. See Peter R. Shergold, *Working-Class Life: The "American Standard" in Comparative Perspective, 1899–1913* (Pittsburgh: University of Pittsburgh Press, 1982).

sylvania, 1872; Ohio, 1877; New Jersey, 1878; Missouri, 1879; Illinois, 1879; Indiana, 1879; New York, 1883; California, 1883; Michigan, 1883; Wisconsin, 1883; Iowa, 1884; Maryland, 1884; Kansas, 1885; Connecticut, 1885; and the "National Bureau," Washington, 1884.

On the value of these reports it is not necessary to dwell. But before passing to the consideration of the results yielded by them two statements may be made. First, these facts, figures, and comments call to mind in the most remarkable way the reports of the English Inspectors under the Factory and Mines Acts. It is impossible to read them without seeing the fatal similarity between the reports from England in the years 1834–66, and those from America of the years 1884–87. He that will compare the abstracts of these too-much-forgotten English reports given in Karl Marx's *Capital* (vol. 1, chap. 10) with the quotations now given, will have no difficulty in seeing how stereotyped are the methods of the system of capitalist production. And he that will compare the picture drawn by F. Engels of the English Working Class in 1844 will see how absolutely parallel are the positions of the English workers in 1844 and of the American in 1887. With this difference. The American has the forty years' experience of his European brethren to teach him, and as Engels says, in America it takes ten months to do what in Europe takes ten years to achieve. Every word of Engels' Introduction, chapter after chapter, page after page of his book, by the simple substitute of "America" for "England" and "American" for "English," apply to the United States of today, and thanks to the higher development of the capitalist system, the concluding words of Engels's work are especially true of the America of our time. "The classes are divided more and more sharply, the spirit of resistance penetrates the workers, the bitterness intensifies, the guerilla skirmishes become concentrated in more important battles, and soon a slight impulse will suffice to set the avalanche in motion."*

The other fact to be noted is that, with one exception, the whole of the Commissioners for the States whose reports we have examined are, as a result of their investigation, in favor of the views advocated by the intelligent of the working class, and opposed by the capitalist class as a body. And this result is not arrived at by any partial, or incomplete, or unfair statement of facts. With one exception, the most scrupulous honesty, and an almost pedantic accuracy of statement, and balancing of evidence are notable. The one exception is that of Mr. Frank A. Flower, the Commissioner for Wisconsin. He, to take but one example, sets an abstract of the opinion of 756 masters against an abstract of opinion of 12 men on the "eight hour" movement. Mr. Flower, of Wisconsin, is also the exception mentioned earlier to the general rule, that the Commissioners endorse the demands that labor is making at the hands of capital.

The evidence to be now given is arranged thus: (1) Evidence of a general nature, necessarily worded with less of precision than is obtainable when actual facts and figures are dealt with; (2) evidence as to the conduct of employers; (3) evidence as to the wages, work, method of living of the employed; (4) evidence as to female and child labor.

In studying this evidence we must remember that it applies almost wholly to the actual workers, and takes no account of the thousands who would work but cannot find anything to do.

---

*Karl Marx, *Capital: A Critique of Political Economy*, vol. 1, translated by Ben Fowkes (New York: Vintage Books, 1977), pp. 340–416; Frederick Engels, *The Condition of the Working Class in England: From Personal Observation and Authentic Sources* [1845; translated by Florence Kelley Wichnewtzky and published in the U.S. in 1887], (Moscow: Progress Publishers, 1973), pp. 333–34.

GENERAL

In this connection we give (a) certain quotations from the various reports on the general condition of the working class; (b) actual statements of comparison between England and America.

(a) *Condition*. Fall River, Massachusetts: "Every mill in the city is making money . . . but the operatives travel in the same old path—sickness, suffering, and small pay." "There is a state of things here that should make men blush for shame." (Physician, p. 204; Cotton Operative, pp. 137–38). "Improved machinery and increased speed, while it increases the manufacturers' profits, and enables the operative to earn more money, yet gives the operative nearly one-third less for his work than formerly; . . . the operatives make more actual money, but they do so much more work for the increased money that they get less per yard than formerly" (Comm., p. 46). "Perhaps any of the evils which exist arise from . . . the increasing tendency to regard the operative simply as a wheel, or a pin to a machine. He is, in the eyes of employers, very much what a mule or spindle is, and no more. . . . It is the fault of the system, not of any man or set of men. They care not who or what the operative is, or where he lives, or what his character, except as any of these things bear on production. They may and do care as men, but not as agents, superintendents, or overseers. . . . We are preparing for New Liverpools, and New Lancashires on American soil, with ignorance, vice, and stupidity as the characteristics of the operative population" (Clergyman's evidence, quoted by Commissioner, pp. 186, 187).

Kansas (State): "Nearly all of our laboring classes here are as badly off as ourselves. What we are to do this winter I don't know. We would be thankful for another railroad wreck, if no one was hurt; it would be a Godsend to all of us" (Plasterer, p. 110). "The wage community in which I live is becoming worse; it is deplorable" (Tinner). "I find that times are getting worse as I grow older" (Teamster). "Corporations must be restrained in some way, or the working people will soon be beggars. I don't see how I am going to live through the winter, as I can get no work at any price" (Plasterer). "For the past seven years things have been growing rapidly worse" (Stonemason). "Work is very much slack at present" (Laborer). "Times are harder now than I ever knew before" (Laborer). "I was raised a slave.... I was better off as a slave" (Farmer, pp. 119–22). "The condition of the laboring classes is too bad for utterance, and is rapidly growing worse" (p. 205). "The depressions existing among our wage-workers" (the Commissioner himself, p. 226). "The condition of the wage-worker is worse than I thought, and deserves to be brought more prominently before the public" (one of the canvassers for the Bureau, p. 259). "It is useless to disguise the fact that out of this ... enforced idleness grows much of the discontent and dissatisfaction now pervading the country, and which has obtained a strong foothold now upon the soil of Kansas, where only the other day her pioneers were staking out homesteads almost within sight of her capital city" (Comm., p. 226). "And it should be bourne in mind that the settlement in Kansas was begun only thirty years ago, and men of middle age vividly recall the fact that this whole region was marked on the schoolboy atlases as the great American desert" (Comm., p. 4).

We purposely give a number of quotations from the Kansas report, as Kansas is one of those fabled Western States as to which the emigrant agents wax eloquent. And in this connection the following facts that came within our personal observation of the much "boomed" Kansas City may be of interest. In districts still quite wild, at least an hour distant from the city, are wretched wooden shanties with three or four rooms. The ground on which these are build cost $600. The "houses" cost another $600, i.e., £240 for three-roomed huts, an hour's distance from the town, roadless, on the top of a bluff, and in a wilderness of mud. And the working men who build or hire these shanties must, in order to do so, mortgage heavily, and then become the mere bond-slaves of the large packing and other corporations that are "running" Kansas City as the "Western Chicago." It is also worth noting that the immense colored population of Kansas is beginning to understand the wage-slavery question. "Their purpose" (i.e., of the "idle classes") "is to keep us poor, so that we shall be compelled to toil for their benefit. I know that our condition is growing rapidly worse, and serious results will surely follow if something is not done. The colored people are getting awake on this matter. The time is past when they can be deceived. They are beginning to think for themselves" (Laborer and Minister, p. 253).

Pennsylvania: "The rich and poor are further apart than ever before" (Commissioner, p. xiii). "The condition of the laboring classes in this city (Pittsburgh) is very bad; their wages are very low; they do not average six dollars a week the year round. Hardly enough to live by" (Glass-blower, p. 133). "I have moved my residence five times during the year 1885, to keep myself in employment" (Coal-miner, Mercer County, p. 165). "I have never experienced such uneasiness in my life as at present, in trying to procure the necessities of life" (Coal-miner, Westmoreland County, p. 164). "I am an American citizen. . . . The miners are not making a decent living by any means, nor could they so if they were working full time at the price now paid. . . . We do not get half a living. . . . We are not paying our way, but going in debt every month" (Miner, Irwin, p. 179).

Michigan: "Labor today is poorer paid than ever before; more discontent exists, more men in despair, and if a change is not soon devised, trouble must come.... I am willing to work as most men are, and now it is time something was done" (Shoemaker in Factory, p. 165). "Employers appear to be trying to ascertain how little a working man can subsist upon, rather than to determine what rate of wages will enable them to procure their wares at the lowest net cost" (Accountant, p. 162).

Ohio: "The American mechanic, subjected as he is to fluctuating extremes of climate, requires a variety of food, and nature has provided it for him; but does he get it in Ohio?... It can hardly be claimed that he does.... Labor-saving machinery has been a blessing to humanity;... but if it has reached the point in development where it forces manual labor into competition with it, how long will it be before it becomes a curse instead of a blessing? The answer must come from the manufacturers themselves. *When man must die* that *trade* may thrive, we have reached the danger line to the republic, and the transition should be sudden and complete" (Comm., pp. 10, 95).

New Jersey: "The struggle for existence is daily becoming keener, and the average wage-laborer must practice the strictest economy, or he will find himself behind at the end of the season" (Comm., p. 142). "I have in former years accumulated considerable, but now... cannot make a cent above expenses" (Locksmith, Newark, p. 220).

(b) *Comparison between England and America*. Fall River: "They are more tyrannical here in Fall River than they are in England. I always thought they were tyrants at home, but found out differently when I came here" (Cotton operative, p. 146). "The universal sentiment was that America, as presented by Fall River, was far behind England in the manner of the treatment of the operatives" (The Commissioner, p. 27).

New Jersey: "I would like to go back to England again, as this country seems to be getting worse every day" (Paterson laborer, p. 228).

Pennsylvania: "I was better off there [Durham, England] than I am here at the present time" (Miner, p. 123). "The wage-laborer is worse off in this country than in England" (Iron-worker, p. 128). "My condition there was as good as it is here. . . . My candid opinion is that the working man in England is as well off as he is here" (Puddler, pp. 129–30). "Six years since I came to this country with wife and five children, . . . was able to pay their way over along with me, and had enough money left . . . to purchase all necessaries for housekeeping, furniture, tools, etc. Today (though some of my family have grown up to help me a little), were I to sell off everything I am possessed of, I could not pay off the debts I owe, much less pay our way back to Europe" (Miner, pp. 130, 131). "My condition was as good there [Wales] as in this country" (Miner, p. 136). "On the whole, I believe, they [in Scotland] are more contented" (Check-weighman, p. 176). "I was in South Wales. Was above my present condition" (Fire-boss, p. 177). "My condition there [Durham] was better than here for the last two years" (Miner, p. 178). "My condition, I think, was better off there [Scotland] than here" (Miner, p. 186). "I came to this country five years ago, and I can say, with a clear conscience, I never was in lower circumstances than I am at present" (Miner, p. 170). On the other hand, one or two miners say they are "better off" in America than in England, but these are, apparently, exceptions to the general rule.

Michigan: "I did not find America as represented to us in England" (Laborer, p. 165).

From the Ohio report we take some very significant passages. They are of a much less general character than all the quotations thus far given, inasmuch as they deal with actual figures with such trifles as wages, working-time, duration of life. "The Ohio moulder earns $80 more than the British moulder,"—but mark the sequel—"he has worked 312 hours, or 35 days longer, to do it. . . . The American moulder dies before he reaches the age of forty, while his British prototype lives to be fifty years and eleven months" (p. 9). As sixteen is the age when in both countries the moulder begins moulding, "the American moulder has twenty-four years to work before death is sure to come, while the British moulder has thirty-five" (p. 9). "In a word, the European workman is a mechanic still, whilst the American workman has ceased to be a mechanic, and has become a machine" (Comm., p. 8).*

---

*The general impressions offered by Aveling and Marx are not inconsistent with the picture drawn by later labor historians. But the realities may be brought into sharper focus if we consult a summary by one of the best of these, David Montgomery. The following can be found on pages 117–18 of his excellent article "Labor in the Industrial Era," in Richard B. Morris, ed., *The U.S. Department of Labor Bicentennial History of the American Worker* (Washington, D.C.: U.S. Government Printing Office, 1976):

> A wide variety of living standards could be found among industrial workers in the latter part of the nineteenth century. It was evident that the gradual increase in real incomes was enjoyed more by some workers than by others. By the end of the 1880s an income of roughly $550 a year would have been necessary for a family of five in a middle-sized industrial town to enjoy any of life's amenities (newspapers, beer, lodge membership, outings, tobacco) without literally depriving themselves of basic necessities. About 40 percent of the working-class families, crowded into one or two rooms in poor tenements, depended heavily on the earnings of children. About one-fourth of them lived in total destitution. Many found their living by scavenging, begging, and hustling.
>
> The largest group of workers (some 45 percent) had incomes which, in good times, clung precariously above the poverty level. Molders, carpenters, machinists, mule spinners, and coal miners might manage a house or flat of four to five rooms (more, if they took in borders) and put plenty of cheaper meat, potatoes, bread, and vegetables on the table, if the mother managed the budget skillfully and the father avoided illness or injury. . . .
>
> Among the most prosperous workers, including many iron rollers, loco-

motive engineers, pattern makers, and glass blowers, incomes ran from $800 to $1,100 yearly. Many union men within this top 15 percent of the working class toiled at tasks both physically exhausting and demanding high levels of experience and judgment. James Parton, a columnist, saw iron craftsmen in Pittsburgh working so hard that they had "to stop, now and then, in summer, take off their boots and *pour the perspiration out of them*."

4 | The Conduct of Employers

All the Old World devices flourish rankly on American soil. Fines, payable in time or money, are exacted.

Lawrence: "If a man or woman stops ten minutes, owing to a break, he or she will have to work twenty minutes' overtime to make up for it" (Cotton operative, p. 117). "If our average is not up to the standard of the mill, we are fined" (Cotton operative, p. 117). We may here say that in all the factory towns of New England that we visited, and notably at Rockville (Conn.), New Bedford (Mass.), and Manchester (New Hampshire), these complaints as to fines were very general. A female "hand" at Rockville and several men at New Bedford assured us that often half their wages in the week went to fines, which were inflicted at the arbitrary whim of the superintendent.

Cheating in the good old-fashioned way, with certain modern improvements, is rife.

Fall River: "The manufacturers take advantage of the length of cuts, and the numbers of the spun yarn" (Commissioner). "The theory is that a 'cut' measures forty-five yards, and for a cut of forty-five yards the weaver is paid, . . . but the cuts in the clothroom as they come from the mill . . . are marked all the way from forty-seven to fifty yards, being a gain or steal of from two to five yards on the part of the corporation" (Former operative, p. 162). The coarser and finer cottons are known as "counts." The pay is higher for, say No. 45 (the finer) than for No. 38 (the coarser). "The overseers let the men spin the 45 counts, and call them 40s, several counts coarser than they really are. . . . This system of cheating costs the spinners about a dollar a week each" (Commissioner, pp. 162–63).

New Jersey: "Thirteen rasps to the dozen are required of me, while the form sells but twelve" (File-cutter, p. 220).

Kansas: This "cheating" goes on in all industries, but probably no one is cheated by his employer so openly and outrageously as the miner. In Kansas, where mining is not yet so developed or flourishing as in Ohio or Pennsylvania, "the miner gets pay for about one-third of his labor, as I know that they (the employers) ship twice as many nut and slack cars as they do lump; and for nut and slack the miner gets nothing, although they sell the slack for two to three cents a bushel, almost as much as they pretend to pay the miner ($3\frac{1}{2}$ cents); and they sell the nut for about four to five cents. They exact eighty-five pounds lump coal from the miner, and sell to their customers eighty pounds to the bushel" (p. 138). "Coal is weighed after it is screened, and the miner gets two parts out of four" (p. 136)

NOTICES TO QUIT

Fall River: "We always require ten days' notice; we have no occasion to give notice, for we discharge at once, without notice, any operative that does not do his work properly." "We always demand ten days' notice, but do not give it; if we want a man to go, he goes." "We give no notice to poor workers, who spoil work, or who are negligent" (p. 136). These three quotations are the answers of the treasurers of three different cotton mills. Working men and women—and not only those employed in mills—constantly complained to us of the arbitrary manner in which their employers discharged them.

BOYCOTTING AND THE BLACK LIST

The virtuous masters hold strong views on the boycott. They also hold strong views on the black list. Unfortunately, the two sets of views are diametrically opposed one to the other. Those of the employers may be gathered from the Wisconsin report.

Wisconsin: "Of the 304 discussing the boycott, 155 think we should have new laws define the practice as a crime, and providing severe penalties for those who engage in it. On the other hand, 149 believe that our present statutes, together with the common-law jurisdiction of courts, are sufficiently comprehensive to deal properly with the subject" (p. 389). Mr. Flower, with his usual spirit of fairness, does not give a single opinion of the workmen on the boycott.

As to the use of the employers' boycott, or the black list, a few quotations.

Fall River: "Nearly all the Fall River operatives visited by the agent seemed to fear the possibility of the manufacturers discovering that they had given information. . . . Thirty members of the Spinners Union were on the black list, and could not obtain work in any mill in the city" (Commissioner, p. 153). The master here quite candidly "own up," as they would say. "We" (says one of them) "started a secret service ... as it gave us the names and occupations of the most prominent in agitating strikes. There have been twenty-six male spinners black-listed since last fall" (p. 155). In Lowell and Lawrence there were no complaints as to the black list. Why? Because of the clever use by the masters of the discharge paper (the equivalent of the French *livret*). "The refusal to grant an 'honorable' discharge to an operative would have the same effect as entering his name on a black list" (Commissioner, p. 156). Method No. 3: "If they leave without a 'line,' at the pleasure of the overseer, their name is given to the agent, and then sent around to all the other corporations, and then there is no more work for that operative" (Correspondent of the Commissioner, p. 210). Two other quotations in this connection as part of the evidence that might be given to show that the black list exists in all States.

Connecticut: "The terrors of the black list, though sometimes exaggerated, have quite enough foundation in fact to make a workman hesitate before braving them." "The real danger [of the black list] ... is to some extent real, and so serious as to make any man hesitate before incurring it. Let any capitalist ask himself candidly what he would do if he were in the workmen's place.... The individual employee ... is at the mercy of the employer" (pp. xxi, xxiii, xxiv).

Michigan: "The working men of Michigan have been invited ... to give us their answers; ... their failure to do so in large numbers may not be from indifference to the subject of labor, so much as from a feeling that possibly their information might expose their identity" (p. 140).

Ohio: "Did his [i.e., the workman who refuses to violate the law by refusing to "truck" payment] hardship end with a discharge, in ordinary times the calamity would not be so serious. If our information be correct a discharge for this reason is a serious matter, for when he seeks employment elsewhere he finds his record, in this respect, precedes him, and unless labor is scarce, he seeks employment in vain" (Commissioner, p. 214).

New York, 1885: "It will be noticed from the testimony on this point that many witnesses assert that they know of their own knowledge that men have been black-listed" (Commissioner, p. 307). The "testimony" referred to by the Commissioner is that of men belonging to well-nigh every possible trade (over twenty in number), from laborers down to journalists.

IRONCLAD OATH

This is a pledge to be taken by the employee on entering service that he will belong to no working-class organization.

New York State: "Considerable complaint is made by the labor organizations of the State, that employers in some sections exact from those seeking work signatures to documents which stipulate that the signer is not, and does not contemplate joining, and will never join, a labor organization" (Commissioner, p. 586).

Here is a copy of an "oath" as drawn up by the Western Union Telegraph Co. of Jay Gould:

I, _____ , of _____ , in consideration of my present re-employment by the Western Union Telegraph Co., hereby promise and agree to and with the said company that I will forthwith abandon any and all membership, connection, or affiliation with any organization or society, whether secret or open, which in any wise attempts to regulate the conditions of

my services or the payment therefore while in the employment now undertaken. I hereby further agree that I will, while in the employ of said company, render good and faithful service to the best of my ability, and will not in any wise renew or re-enter upon any relations or membership whatsover in or with any such organization.
      Dated, _____ 1883. Signed, _____
       Address _____ . (Seal). (p. 587)

"At the time of the plumbers' strike in June 1884 the following pledge was drawn up, and the men asked to sign it: 'I, _____ , do hereby solemnly declare that I am not a member of any journeymen's organization, and that I will not in the future join or become a member of any of the now existing journeymen's organizations. To the truthfulness of the foregoing declaration I hereby pledge my word and honor as a man'" (p. 587). "To the employees of the Warren Foundry. . . . We request every man who has joined the above organization (Knights of Labor) and wishes to continue in employ of the Warren Foundry to immediately free himself from a combination hostile to the company. . . . If there are any not willing to do so, we request them to leave our premises. . . . Anyone not willing to conform to the above requests . . . will be summarily discharged. . . . Signed _____ , President, _____ , Superintendent" (Phillipsburg, 7 April 1885, New Jersey Report, p. 220).

A personal reminiscence here may be indulged. In Springfield, Ohio, one William Whiteley (oddly enough) owns, with his brothers, nearly everything; the shops for the making of agricultural implements the bodies of most of the working population, and their political souls. He is a great man on the ironclad oath. All his men take it and break it. He has placarded in his workshops offers of a ten-dollar reward to any workman who will give information as to a fellow-workman belonging to a labor organization. Over the entrance to his chief shop are the words, "Free and independent workmen only employed here."

On November 9 we were at the little town of Bloomington, Ill. Two of the most earnest of the many working men who helped in the announcement and noising abroad of the meeting in the Opera House at which we spoke, Eberding and Kronau, were, within a few hours of our leaving Bloomington, dismissed by their employers. They were noted as industrious, honest, sober men, and as two of the best workmen in the place. Their crime was taking an open interest in lectures on the condition of the working classes.

THE "TRUCK," "ORDER," OR "SCRIP" SYSTEM

This system, as they sometimes call it in America, exists to a larger extent, and in more openly brutal fashion, than in any part of Great Britain.

Ohio: "The man who compels his employee to take 'scrip' in payment of wages violates the statute" (p. 216). Of course, "no direct compulsion is used, but, nevertheless, should an employee refuse or neglect to patronize the company's store, a hint is conveyed to him, in a roundabout way, that his prospects at the mine would be vastly improved by trading at the store of his employer. If this has not the desired effect, he is laid off for a few days, and then the hint is renewed, with the addition that this is the last chance. This failing, the next move is to make the miner's position unpleasant by a system of persecution that life becomes a burden. Upon the finishing up of his room he is told there is no more work for him" (Miner, Shawnee, Perry County, p. 214). Here we may further add that in many cases, as the land and houses are also the property of the "corporations," there are only "corporation stores"; and, to quote Mr. McHugh, the Commissioner for Ohio, "As some of them [i.e., employers] frankly confess, *to cut off the profits of the store would destroy the most profitable part of their business*" (Ohio Report, p. 217).

Kansas: "Most of the miners have a company store, and if the miner don't do all his trading with them he is discharged. . . . The miner has to rent of the company, trade with the company, and be idle when they don't want him to work. If this is not slavery, what is it? . . . Once get a miner here, and get him in debt to them and they own him. If he has a family he can't get enough ahead to get away" (Miner, Crawford, p. 38).

Michigan: "The greatest difficulty that the wage worker has to contend with, in my opinion, is the custom of many firms doing business on what is called the 'white horse' plan—that is, *orders*" (Machinist, p. 161). "The order system, which is in vogue in north of the State, . . . is nothing but a system of robbery" (Carpenter, p. 161). "I could take the cash and go among the farmers, and buy what they have to sell for one-third, and sometimes one-half what we have to pay the company. My book account at the store shows one dollar per bushel for potatoes, which did not cost the company more than twenty five cents" (Saw Mill Laborer, pp. 161–62). "I worked all last summer in same shop as at present, and only received thirty dollars in cash during the entire year" (Cooper, p. 162). "I have tried the store-order system, and have proved by actual figures that I can buy for 30 percent less than for orders" (Marble Cutter, p. 162)

Pennsylvania: "We have a company's store here, and are expected to deal in it" (Miner, Allegheny County, p. 123). "The company's stores, where nearly all the employees are compelled to deal. . . . The reason I said 'if there is anything due' is because the company deducts the store bill, rent, doctor [the company deducts seventy-five cents per month for medicine and medical attendance], coal, etc., from the men. It is seldom a married man has any pay to get, especially an outside laborer" (Laborer, Carbon County, pp. 152, 153).

Trusteeing is another form of this robbery of the employed by the employer. It is practically a mortgaging of wages to a shopkeeper for goods supplied. How this reacts on man and master may be seen from two quotations.

Fall River: "When a man is trusteed twice he is discharged, because it causes the bookkeeper trouble and the agent is apt to imagine the man is dishonest. Then they take every cent of his money here" (Cotton Operative, p. 20). "The system enables the laborer to get credit—at exorbitant prices—and so live ahead of his earnings; second, the lawyers in Lowell add their fee to the cost, and collect it of the defendant, which is contrary to law" (p. 208).

VIOLATIONS OF THE LAWS

In America, as in England, the employer does not scruple to break all or any of the laws for the protection of the laborer. "Laws in several states have been passed, aiming at the removal of the truck and Company-store system. . . . There is yet, however, too much evasion of these laws" (First Annual Report but the Commissioner of Labor, Washington, p. 244).

Ohio: "We have personally and by letter caused complaints to be made to the prosecuting attorneys in four counties of the State, where flagrant violation of this law [i.e., concerning the truck system] were of almost hourly occurrence, and with the exception of Perry Country, so far as we are advised, not one case of this kind has been made the subject of investigation by grand juries. . . . If a hungry man steals a ham, and forces a lock or pries open a door to do it, it is burglary, and a prosecuting attorney will take special delight in having him sent to the penitentiary for it; but for the man who pays his men in 'scrip' and thus indiscriminately robs the helpless families of his employees, prosecuting attorneys have 'nought but smiles and pleasant greetings,' as though those upon whom these men were depredating were entitled to no protection, and wealth could do no wrong" (Comm., p. 216).

Fall River: "There should be a compliance by the large manufacturing establishments with the ten-hour law, which has never yet been enforced" (Correspondence of Commissioner, p. 190). "A member of a city Board of Health ordered a wealthy house owner to abate a nuisance in a tenement block. The owner paid no attention until the order was made imperative. Then, instead of complying with the law, he visited the other members of the board, and said that the first member was persecuting him, and letting others go who were just as bad. By a vote of two to one he was given six months more time" (Commissioner, p. 72).

Connecticut: "There are, in the United States today, a great many instances of laws unenforced. . . . Violation of the foreign contract labor law . . . go on from month to month" (Commissioner, p. xxi). These violations of the law by the law-makers are most frequent in mines, for the sufficient reason that these are the working places most out of sight. "We see them [the Labor Laws] violated every day, and no penalty inflicted for violating the same" (Miner, p. 125).

Pennsylvania: "Others [i.e., companies] are shielding themselves behind the technicality that the miners have not requested them individually to send in their props, also giving length, number, and size of the required props. I think this is a poor excuse, as the meaning of the law undoubtedly is that all companies and parties interested shall live up to its spirit" (Commissioner, p. 137a). In this same report there are some half-dozen terrible lists of accidents to miners, and the majority of these would not have occurred had the laws been carried out by the masters and overseers.

One of the main reasons why labor laws are thus violated is, in America as in England, the small number of Inspectors. "Laws do not execute themselves," writes Mr. McHugh. "A law ... proved to be inoperative owing to no public official being especially required to enforce it.... We do not believe that any inspector can make four proper inspections to each mine yearly" (Comm., p. 80b). "We are told there is a mine Inspector somewhere in Kansas" (says a Kansas witness, p. 138 of the Report), "but unless Governor Glick saw him come and draw his pay, I know that he was not seen in his official capacity by any miner in Leavenworth." It is satisfactory to learn from the Commissioner that since this statement was made the Leavenworth miners "have seen the mine Inspector in his official capacity." Complaints of a like nature were made to us in factory towns in New England, in mining districts like LaSalle, Illinois, and in New York State.

Summing up the whole question of this violation of laws, the Ohio Commissioner says: "We, in America, boast of our superiority in the freedom and democracy of our institutions, and our respect for the laws made by the representatives of the people, and that all laws regularly enacted are entitled to obedience and respect until declared unconstitutional by the courts.... But if the manner in which the scrip law in Ohio is enforced and respected should be taken as evidence against us, would we not have to hang our heads in shame, and acknowledge that our boasted veneration for law is but a sham and a delusion, and that statutes that put a curb on our cupidity have no binding force or effect, and were only enacted for the purposes of pandering to a sentiment?" (Comm., p. 228).

Wherever there is any difficulty in getting information for the Bureaux of Labor, the masters are its cause. Either the men are afraid of the black list if they tell the truth, or the masters actually refuse to give any information to the Commissioners. Ohio: "Many of those who refuse to give information asked by the Bureau are corporate companies, who owe their existence to, and are maintained and protected in every right by, a law enacted by the same power that created the Bureau. They preach law, but do not practice it, and the Bureau is powerless to compel them to do so" (Commissioner, p. 150).

As final evidence of the moral tone of the employers, two last quotations. Fall River: "This feeling [of national antagonism] is fostered by the manufacturers in the belief that by causing dissensions among the help [hands] it would interfere with their joining hands on any question of labor reform" (Commissioner, p. 14). Pennsylvania: "It is not the widows and orphans that are the masters' chief concern [in employing children], but rather their zealous worship of the almighty dollar" (Commissioner, p. 80b).

5 | Wages, Work, Method of Living

A. WAGES

The wages of the American laborer, as measured in terms of money, are generally higher than in England. Against this, however, must be set the greater expense of living and rent, the longer working hours, and above all the greater intensity of labor in America. With each of these we shall deal directly. Here, therefore, only one or two general notes on the amount of wage, and especially on the time of payment.

Fall River: "The average wage in Fall River is $9 a week. For a single man . . . this is scarcely sufficient" (Commissioner, p. 28).

Kansas: "It is hard work to earn $1 per day" (Tailoress, p. 118) "A man with a family working, as I have to, for $1.25 per day can barely live" (Laborer, p. 118). "It will be seen that the highest daily average wages paid any one trade . . . is to bricklayers . . . yearly earnings $425. . . . Stone cutters average next highest . . . yearly earning $415.71. . . . Iron servants $511.11." "The average annual earnings . . . as a fair average of the general earnings throughout the State, $333.09." Michigan: "Average wages paid to 549 persons, $1.67 per day" (Commissioner, p. 141).

Our own inquiries in the lumber districts showed that the average wage per day was 40 to 90 cents, the average time of employment six months in the year.

Pennsylvania: "Average highest wages to miner, $2 per day, ... laborers $1.40, boys 50 to 60 cents per day. Idle Days, 111" (Comm. p. 8a). "I will risk my life on the assertion that the last figures ($270 wages for the year to miners, Somerset County) are at least 10 percent above the average earnings in this region, except one mine" (p. 170).

New Jersey: "The daily wages for skilled miners $1.20 to $1.55; for ordinary labor $1 to $1.25; boys 55 to 75 cents. ... In some of our mines the wages during the year were reduced to 90 cents per day" (Commissioner, pp. 281, 291). "My actual earnings last year were but $100, while the cost of living was $400" (Paterson, p. 227). "Wages have been reduced 50 percent, in three years" (Silkworker, p. 226). The average wage throughout the United States, according to the last census, was $1.15 per worker per day, a sum which every one to whom we spoke, employers and employed alike, declared wholly insufficient to "keep a family" in the States. And we should bear in mind that this "average" includes some exceptionally well-paid men, and takes no account of the thousands of unemployed who would work if they could. The New York Commissioner touches the heart of the question of wagers in the following passage: "While the fixing of wages is left to the employer alone, ... the only limit to reduction is starvation" (p. 611).

One great source of grievance among the workers lies in the fact that in many cases the wages are paid not only weekly but fortnightly or monthly.

Kansas: "Employees are kept out of their pay for too long a

period, especially by railroad corporations.... Most ... of the railroad companies keep back from fifteen to twenty days' pay" (Tinsmith, p. 118). "A man ... has to wait 50 days before he receives a cent of wages, and then he only gets pay for 30 days, leaving the proceeds of twenty days' labor in the company's hands till he quits their employ" (Railroad Laborer, p. 119). "I find that the amount of wages thus retained from month to month by the companies is reported as representing from fifteen to twenty days' labor.... The poorest paid and most numerous class ... are thus unable to exist from pay-day to pay-day without credit" (Commissioner, p. 228).

Michigan: "Of 520 laborers asked, 'Are you paid weekly, fortnightly, or monthly?' 146 answered weekly, 32 fortnightly, 177 monthly, 28 whenever I want it, 137 no regular pay-day" (Commissioner, p. 151). "'How long are wages withheld?' 'A week to ten days' (Mason). 'Sixty to ninety days' (Laborer). 'One month' (Fireman). 'Ninety days' (Carpenter, laborer, farm-laborer). 'Sometimes three months' (Engineer). 'As long as they are able to keep it' (Machinist). "Six months to a year' (Single sawyer). 'Seven months' (Sawmill laborer). 'Sometimes for life' (Carpenter)" (pp. 152, 153).

Connecticut: "Of the factory operatives a little less than two-fifths are paid weekly, a little more than two-fifths monthly, most of the others fortnightly" (p. ix). In Pennsylvania monthly payments prevail in the coal regions, elsewhere fortnightly. "When one starts to work it is sometimes seven weeks before he gets any pay" (Miner, p. 163).

B. WORKING TIME

As to the length of this per day, let us take the State of Connecticut as a fair general type of the New England cotton factories, which have been, to some extent, influenced by legislation. Of 65,627 hands . . . about 5 percent were employed 54 hours (per week); a little over 22 percent from 55 to 59; over 56 percent, 59.5 or 60 hours; "12 percent of the men, 22 percent of the women, and 34 percent of the children are employed more than 10 hours daily. On the other hand, 30 percent of the men, 28 percent of the women, and only 11 percent of the children are employed less than 10 hours daily" (Comm., p. xv). New England: "In England, they [silk workers] work only 54 hours, here we have 60" (Silk-worker, Patterson, p. 226).

One or two special cases taken from other callings. Fall River: "Tram-drivers 15 hours per day. Kansas street car conductors 16 and 17 hours a day. But the most unfortunate of these wretched car-servants are the drivers of the so-called 'bob-tail' cars. On these there are no conductors, and the one man not driving, be it remembered, as, for example, the Blackfriars Bridge Cars, a short and stated distance, but often from one end of a town to another has to drive, collect money, give change, stop for the passengers who wish to alight or who wish to ascend, keep his accounts 'made up,' and this for 16 to 18 hours a day. And for such hard work the men do not get enough, as a Milwaukee driver told us, to 'keep their families.'" New York: Bakers $16\frac{2}{3}$ hours for 6 days; they always, without exception, work Sunday; it amounts to $14\frac{5}{28}$ per day" (p. 327). Wisconsin: "Laborer, on the Menominee River, 15 to 17 hours per day." Pennsylvania: "Here I see men working 14, 16, and 18 hours, and I know that some of them go into the mines on Sunday, trying to make a living and cannot, while their employers own Sunday-schools, churches, preachers, Government bonds, ... with yachts, steamboats, orange plantations, and are very rich" (Iron-worker, p. 128). "We worked 6 hours per day in England, here we work from 10 to 12 hours a day" (Miner, p. 160). "In England ... there is more leisure time for culture" (Miner, p. 145). "In England I worked 6 hours per day, ... here a miner ... has to work all the hours God sends in fact, make a beast of himself or starve" (p. 131).

The eight-hour working day is declared for with a practical unanimity by the working men and by the Commissioners. In the Kansas report the answers from the men belonging to 18 different trades are given. They all declare for shorter hours of work, and 12 of the 18 for an eight-hour day. Wisconsin: Of the 12 men against the 756 masters, 10 are for 8 hours, 1 for 9 hours, and 1 against reduction. Of the 756 masters, 437 were against the reduction of the working day to 8 hours, 68 were for it, 20 indefinite, 233 silent. New York: "The most remarkable feature of the investigation in New York City was the unanimity with which the witnesses answered interrogations in regard to shorter hours of labor. They invariably expressed themselves in favor of shortening the working day" (p. 515). The Pennsylvania Commissioner will make a good end to this set of quotations: "That eight hours will in the not distant future be the standard measure of a day's work is, in my opinion, beyond doubt" (p. 15).

In America, as in England, a large number of the working men are in enforced idleness through part of the year. We are not speaking here of the great army of the perennially unemployed, but of those who would be said even by the capitalist class to be workers.

Kansas (Miners): "This mine has probably worked half-time during the year." "At present we are working half-time" (p. 136).

"A printer whose lost time during the last years was six months" (p. 204). A colored woman, seamstress: "My husband is over one-half his time idle through inability to get work" (p. 206). A summary on page 258 shows that in Topeka, in 1885, of 660 skilled workmen, 156 worked only part of the time, 108 had no work; of 372 laborers 77 worked only part of the time, 113 had no work. "Skilled and unskilled workmen . . . out of employed . . . over 1 in 5" (p. 259). Important figures, since we are constantly told both in Europe and America that "skilled labor" is always certain of employment "out West."

New Jersey: "The locomotive works in Paterson, at one time employing 3,500 men, has not given work to 500 during the last year and a half. Many of the ironworkers, machinists, blacksmiths, etc., could be seen around the city hose-house, . . . trying to get a few weeks' work on the streets. . . . But there were always four times more than were necessary" (p. 218).

Michigan: "I am out of employment so long that I am sick and tired of looking for work" (Machinist). "I am willing to do any kind of work, but am unable to secure work at any price" (Carpenter). "Cannot get employment only about two or three days in a week" (Painter). "I only had a very little work last summer" (Laborer). "My position as a wage-worker is rather blue at present, because there are so many men that are out of employment" (Wood-worker). "Am out of work at present, and no prospect of any work" (p. 160).

We quote from the report on "Industrial Depression": "Out of the total number of establishments, such as factories, mines, etc., existing in the country during the year ending July 1, 1885, 7.5 percent . . . were idle or equivalent to idle. . . . There were in round numbers 255,000 such establishments employing upwards of 2,250,000 hands. . . . Then there were possibly 19,125 establishments idle or equivalent to idle, 168,750 hands out of employment, so far as such establishments were concerned during the year considered" (p. 65).

To the displacement of human by machine labor not a little of this enforced "idleness" is due. How many skilled workers have, during the last few years, been driven into the ranks of the unskilled and unemployed in America, will be better appreciated from the following facts—taken from Colonel Wright's Report on Industrial Depressions, 1886, pp. 80–86—than from anything we could ourselves say on the subject. In the manufacture of agricultural implements, during the last 15 or 20 years, machinery has displaced "fully 50 percent of muscular labor." In manufactures of small arms displacement of 44 to 49 men in one "operation." Boots and shoes . . . in some cases, 80 percent displaced, in others 50 to 60. "Within the past 30 years," says one Philadelphia manufacturer, "machinery has displaced about 6 times the amount of hand labor required." Broom industry, 50 percent. Carriages and wagons, 34 percent. Carpets, weaving, spinning, and all the processes together, displaced 10 to 20 times the number of persons now necessary. . . . In spinning alone 75 to 100 times the number. Hats, displacement, 9 to 1. Cotton goods, within 10 years, 50 percent (in New Hampshire). Flour, nearly three-fourths of the manual labor displaced. Furniture, one-half to three-fourths. Leather-making, 50 percent. Metals, and metallic goods, one man with one boy can produce as much as was formerly produced by 10 skilled men. One boy running a planing machine does the work of 25 men. In the Hocking Valley, mining coal by machines, 160 men do the work of 500. Oil industry, Penn., 5,700 teams of horses, and double that number of men, displaced. Wall paper, displacement 100 to 1. Railroad supplies, 50 percent. Silk manufacture, general manufacture, 40 percent; weaving, 95, winding, 90. Woollen goods: carding, 33 percent; spinning, 50; weaving, 25. "This is during the last few years only . . . machinery in spinning and weaving has displaced 20 times the hand labor formerly employed.

The stealing of the employees' time goes on just as criminally in America as in this country. Fall River: "An operative said, '. . . if the superintendent takes ten minutes in the morning, fifteen at noon, and five at night, it is nobody's business' " (p. 109). "Clocks have been put back half an hour, and where a mill with 2,000 looms does a thing of this kind the steal amounts to something" (Former Operative, p. 109). "As a rule, they [the spinners] all go into the mill half an hour before starting-up time . . . then at noon they must clean up, and that takes all the dinner hour, so that they rarely get out of the mill during the day" (p. 115). This "stealing on time" is the "nibbling and cribbling of time" denounced in England by Leonard Horner. (See *Capital*, p. 226.)*

C. INTENSIFICATION OF LABOR

This, more than anything, distinguishes the American laborer from the British. Every one of the many working men and women of every calling that had come from England, to whom we spoke in America, laid stress on the fact that the workers in the New World had to do more work in a given time. "Until I came here," said one of them, "I did not know what hard work was"; and our friend P. J. McGuire, one of the most experienced and active labor organizers, told us that it usually "took months" before the British worker could be "broken into the style of work in

---

*Page 351 of 1977 Vintage Books edition.

America." They must keep up an awful strain or drop out of the race. Fall River: "I saw on the sheet in a certain mill, written opposite the name of a female weaver, 'a lazy weaver,' and opposite another, '5½ cuts, or get out' " (p. 113). "We used to get off twenty-eight thousand in a week, now we get off thirty-three thousand under the ten-hour law" (p. 47). Ohio: "By having the work made . . . at such prices . . . a moulder would be obliged to do two days' work for one day's wages" (Superintendent, Machine Shop, p. 10). "The 'hurry and push' that has been introduced of late years into the American workshops" (p. 10). "In fact, the workers state that the 'grinding' or 'driving' . . . was almost beyond human endurance" (Fall River, p. 156).

D. METHOD OF LIVING

A few words on the horrors of the tenement houses. New York City is especially the home of these dens. New York: In 1883 there were 25,000 tenement houses, with 1,000,000 inhabitants. As to the overcrowding, it is estimated that 18,996 tenement houses accommodate fifty people each, and not a few of these contain three times as many. "I have seen a family of six and even eight people living in the customary front and 'inside' room. Where they all slept was a mystery, but that a portion of them were obliged to sleep on the floor seemed the only explanation. The temperature of these rooms is excessive, and while the smell of sewer gas is in itself obnoxious, it becomes simply refreshing when compared with the stifling fumes that seem to permeate every nook and corner of these dilapidated tenements. They cook, eat, and sleep in the same room, men, women, and children together. Refuse of every description makes the floors damp and slimy, and the puny, half-naked children crawl or slide about in it" (Commissioner, pp. 174, 179). "These people very seldom cooked any of their meals. . . . I have seen large accumulations of tobacco scraps and tobacco stems which, having long lain in that way, have become putrid; in one instance I ran the point of my shoe into a mass of this kind to see what it really was, and it was filled with vermin" (Evidence of Cigar Maker on Tenement House Cigar Factories, Report for 1884, p. 154).

In other towns and cities besides New York City, both in New York and other States, the like is to be see. Pennsylvania: "I know of forty people living in a little house of three rooms. It is a common thing for seven people to live in one room" (p. 128). Fall River: "The Granite Mills houses were the best in the city" and yet "sixteen houses use the same privy, and the stench in summer is unbearable" (Weaver, p. 81). "The inhabitants of Norombega Black (Lowell, Mass.) have to carry their refuse of all kinds, and human excrements, save when they throw it between the two blocks . . . into Austin Avenue for deposit" (Comm., p. 91). "These tenements are . . . bad, morally as well as in a sanitary point of view" (p. 84). "The tenements throughout the city are in a very poor condition" (Cotton Spinner, p. 80). " 'Dirty,' 'foul odors,' 'wretched and dirty,' 'excessively filthy,' such are the terms in which the Commissioner speaks of the Fall River tenements. Some of the very worst are those owned by the corporations, and the 'hands' are forced to live in them." "When a man is employed by a mill he is compelled to move into their tenements. Their breakfast depends on their moving in, and their life on their moving out. The recent strike at the Chace Mills was caused by the refusal of a newly engaged man to move out of a private tenement and into one of the company's. He did not consider it fit to live in, so refused, and was discharged, and for no other reason" (p. 84).

For these "filthy," "dirty," "wretched" houses exorbitant rents are charged. And as to the landlords of these miserable dwelling: "It would seem," says the New York Commissioner, "as if a spirit common humanity would prompt the owners of such property to prevent a continuance of these awful health-destroying and disease-infecting cesspools.... Humanity, however, has little or nothing to do with the case. The main and all-important question with these people seems to be to get the largest possible revenue from their wretched rookeries with the least possible outlay" (New York Report, 1886, p. 177). "The Harris Block on Hall Street (Lowell) is owned by a man who gives his name to the block, and in the census of 1880 it was found that in the 36 tenements there were 396 persons in the 36 families.... The owner of the block pays a ground rent of $260 per year, and receives an average rental from each tenement of $8; the total for one month, $288, more than covering his yearly land rent" (Fall River, Comm., p. 92). "They are not as good as we would like to have them, but good enough for the operatives" (Cotton Manufacturer, p. 83).

As to the question of food. The verbal testimony of the English in America to us was always in effect that food cost as much in America as in England, or more in America than in England. But there is another aspect of this question generally forgotten: that is, not what the food costs, but what can the laborer afford to spend per day upon it. Ohio: "Wards of the State [the people in the punitive, reformatory, and benevolent institutions] cost for subsistence per head $0.1683 per day. For the purpose of subsistence the working people spend $0.139 per day per person" (p. 95). Of course, in the former case the food is bought wholesale, and in the latter retail.

The food question leads to that of drink. In America, as in England, there are not wanting people, even among the working classes, who, confusing effects and causes, explain the miserable condition of the workers by the fact that they will drink. Of sixteen Kansas laboring men, seven declare for temperance as necessary if the cause of labor is to succeed, and four others are anxious for prohibition. A wagon-maker says, however, "I don't think this howl about the working man spending so much for whiskey is truthful. . . . I am confident that the proportion is much less than it is among any other class—businessmen, for instance." A printer puts the matter in the right light. "I will admit that we should preach and practice temperance, but there are other evils that we have got to fight" (pp. 120, 121). A doctor, quoted in the Fall River Report, takes what Colonel Carroll Wright calls "a more philosophical view of the cause and the tendency of the evil." "I must admit that the system of overworking the operatives is so debilitating as to seem to make necessary the use of some kind of stimulant, and could that necessity be met by a very moderate use of beer and spirits all might be well" (p. 176). Say the Cotton Operatives: "The 'drive' they are subjected to leads them to take a stimulant in order to recuperate their energies" (p. 62).

6 | Woman and Child Labor

The employment of the labor of women and children has, in America as in England, two chief causes that react one on the other. By their employment the capitalist obtains labor at a cheaper rate, and the poverty of the laborer's family forces the weaker members of it to seek for work. "And this employment of women and child labor has assumed alarming proportions, relatively larger . . . than in Europe" (New Jersey Report, p. 265).

The employer prefers to employ women and children.

Fall River: "We never employ men when we can get women who can do their work just as well. This is done, not only on account of the reduced expenses, but because they cause less trouble by striking, or by finding unnecessary fault" (Superintendent, p. 122). A Lawrence weaver said: "One of the evils existing in this city is the gradual extinction of the male operative. . . . Within a radius of two squares in which I am living, I know of a score of young men who are supported by their sisters and their mothers, because there is no work in the mills for them" (p. 11).

New Jersey: "Woman and child labor is much lower priced

than that of men, . . . the hours of labor are longer and the rate of wages less, women never agitate, they merely 'toil and scrimp, and bear' " (New Jersey Report, 1884, Commissioner, p. 265). "Women, however, are learning that they must agitate, and that the highest virtue is not to 'scrimp, and toil, and bear.' " According to the just-issued New Jersey Report, "Since the girls have joined the Knights of Labor here (Vineland) they make the same wages as the men" (Commissioner Report, 1886, p. 188). In some cases the women are certainly employed on work of too arduous a nature.

Pennsylvania: "That women have been permitted to perform the severe manual labor generally apportioned to men [in mines] is true. . . . The owners did not directly hire the women, but must have been cognizant of the facts" (Commissioner, B.).

Women's time is stolen and their lives risked like those of men.

Utica, New York State: "Question: 'Was it not the custom to go in before the starting time to clean machinery?' Answer (female weaver): 'Yes, sir, it was.' Question: 'Did you get paid extra for it?' Answer: 'No, sir; and the girls used to clean their looms while running, at the risk of getting their hands taken off' " (New York, 1884, p. 127). When they are employed at work for which they are supposed to be fitted the wages are terribly low.

New York (Report for 1885): "An expert [at crocheting ladies' shawls] could earn $12\frac{1}{2}$ cents for a day's labor." "The half-starved, overworked seamstress . . . pays for the machine by which . . . she is enabled to make pants for $1.50 a dozen. Vests at 15 cents a piece. It is this slave-ridden and driven woman that, in case of fire, is held responsible for the goods that may be destroyed in her awful rookery home." Collar and cuff makers, "Women pay out of their wages about $75 per year for thread." Tailoress earns "four months a year $3 per week. The place is in horrible condition." Shirt ironers, wages $1.25 to $1.50 per week. Gloves per dozen, 90 cents, "Millinery, 12 cents a day.... Firm pays every two weeks." The law demands that in certain occupations seats shall be provided for the women employed. The seats are provided—but "the spirit of the law is absolutely defied, and set at nought by the refusal of employers to allow these women to occupy them." In America, as in England, the sweater "lives on the woman's earnings, literally on her sweat and blood." Ladies' undergarments, 30 cents per dozen; small size, 15 cents per dozen. Wrappers, $1 per dozen. Cloak working, women employed by the great dry goods stores—full day's pay—... 50 to 60 cents.... Shirts, 75 cents to $1.50 per dozen. Of 1,322 women, 27 earned $6 a week; 6 earned $5; 127 earned $4; 534 earned $1. Women in factories are fined on every possible pretext. If found with a paper in their hands, sometimes as high as $2, and for being late as much as $1. There is no fixed amount, whatever may occur to the foreman or superintendent.... Fines for being five minutes late, in a silk weaving factory 25 cents, and half hour's time; for washing your hands 25 cents; eating a piece of bread at your loom $1; also for imperfect work, sitting on a stool, taking a drink of water, and many trifling things too numerous to mention."

Matters are just as bad in other large cities as in New York. For instance in Philadelphia, ladies' wrappers are made for 60 cents per dozen. The best wages paid do not go beyond $5 per week. Plain jerseys bring 37 cents per dozen, the maximum earning per week reaching $4. Overalls are made for 5 cents a pair; an active worker can turn out ten pairs a day. Long aprons, called "nurse aprons," with a deep hem all around and two tucks at the bottom, bring 35 cents a dozen. By working from 5:30 in the morning till 7 at night, two dozen can be made in a day. The average wages paid to saleswomen and girls employed in clerical work does not exceed $5 per week. On this they have to dress well in order to keep their position. Board and room at the lowest figure is $3, not counting laundry work, which has also to come from the $5. The sanitary conditions of the workshops and factories is described as very bad, and "calls for immediate reform." In many factories where men and women are employed there are no separate closets for the women, and many modest girls risk their health on this account. The 'hands' are *locked* into the rooms. We ourselves were shown such a room where a number of unhappy girls had been burnt to death through such locking of the doors."

Of the "peculiar abuses" to which these women are subject a few are mentioned by the Commissioner: "Artificial flowers: Poisoned hands and cannot work. Had to sue the man for 50 cents." Saleswoman: "No ventilation and have to use gas or electric light all day." Shoes: "Water in fire buckets is not often changed. It is frequently green with age." Gents' ties: "Work in basement with gas light." "One hundred women and small girls work in a cellar without ventilation, and electric light burning all day." "In certain workshops there are facilities for washing, but if caught washing fined" (Comm., pp. 147–62).

If the workshops and factories are in this condition, it will easily be imagined what the "homes" and the "house-labor" of these women are like. "No words of mine," Mr. Peck says, speaking of the tenements and their female occupants, "certainly can convey to the public any adequate conception of the truly awful condition of thousands of these suffering people" (p. 164). "A room on the attic floor of a wretched old rookery in Hester Street . . . was possibly ten feet square. The ceiling was low and slanting, and its only source of light was through the begrimed panes of glass of a small gable window opening on the roof. . . . The air was stifling . . . and odoriferous with sewer gas. Piled upon the floor were stacks of cloaks ready to be put together. The women (a number of cloak makers) were scantily clad, their hair was unkempt, and their pale, abject countenances, as they bent over their work, formed a picture of physical suffering and want, that I had certainly never seen before.... They were working as if driven by some unseen power; but when I learned that they were enabled to earn 50 cents for sixteen and perhaps more hours' labor per day, it needed no further investigation to convince me that the 'unseen power' was the necessity of bread for their own and their children's mouths. The style and quality of the cloaks upon which these women were at work was of the latest and best. They were lined with quilted silk or satin, and trimmed with sealskin or other expensive material, and found ready sale in the largest retail stores of the city, at from $35 to $75 each. Two of these women could manage by long hours and most diligent application to turn out one cloak per day, and the price received was $1, or 50 cents apiece. This," adds the Commissioner, "is not a fancy picture nor is it an exceptional case." In another such room where also the "temperature was next to suffocating and dense with impurities... on one end of the table, at which four of these women sat, was a dinner pail, partially filled with soup—that is what they called it—and a loaf of well-seasoned bread. These two sumptuous courses, served with one spoon and one knife, satiated the thirst and hunger of four working women." A trained seamstress said: "I have sat steadily at the machine from six o'clock in the morning till one o'clock at night—and I sew rapidly—and yet only make 25 cents a day."

But "the most deplorable aspect of woman's labor is to be found among those unfortunates who, having no specific calling, are forced to seek casual labor... at scrubbing or washing.... Visits have been made to these women's resorts of which it can only be said that the condition of debasement is beyond description if not belief. . . . In a single tenement house on the West Side of New York . . . a building five stories in height, very narrow, and with an extremely shabby exterior. The main entrance was not over three feet in width, and the stairs were uncomfortably steep, and hardly admitted of the passage of two persons. They were lighted (?) from a very small and dirty skylight set in the roof, and barely discernable by reason of the accumulated cobwebs and dust of generations. . . . The case of one family found living on the fifth or attic floor was of a character to touch even the most hardhearted. My knock on the door was responded to by the feeble voice of a middle-aged man, who, upon entering, I found sitting on an old box close to the broken-down stove which stood, or rather was propped up by bricks, at one side of the apartment. He was engaged in whittling a small stick with which to kindle a fire, while three children hovered near by, and seemed chilled with cold. The furniture of the room, if I might dignify it by that name, consisted of a pine table, three legs of which were made from rough pieces of board, one of these even being spliced; the fragments of what had originally been two chairs, and the remains of an old sofa, with its hind legs intact, and the place of the two missing ones in front supplied with chunks of wood. This room was possibly ten feet square, and lighted by a single window, which gave a view of the walls of a large factory which hemmed in the tenement on two sides. Connected with this was the almost universal 'inside' room absolutely without ventilation or light, except that gained through the door opening into it. Its cramped space was nearly taken up with a bed consisting of a filthy old mattress, stretched out on the top of two old trunks, and a wooden box. From conversation with the man I learned the fact that he was a cripple and unable to work. In addition to the three children present he had two older ones, . . . and these seven human beings lived in these two rooms. . . . This was but one of perhaps twenty family histories in the same building. . . . In this same building was the home of another scrub-woman; . . . the woman was in poor health, . . . and the features of her one child at home—a little girl some five years of age—looked pale, pinched, and forlorn; her emaciated body was covered with an aggregation of rags, . . . the two formed a sad and touching picture. And all within a stone's throw of Broadway, the great business thoroughfare of New York City. . . . It must be understood that they are not abandoned women, but are really working women" (pp. 165–67).

The condition of the women employed in cigar-making (i.e., in tenements) is on all fours with the above. Just as the cloak makers "work till twelve or one o'clock, sleep by the machine a few hours, and then commence to work again" (p. 178), these women also, with their families, "work, eat, and sleep in these rooms." "I see women," says a thoroughly reliable witness, "surrounded by filth with children waddling in it, and having sores on their hands and faces and various parts of the body. . . . They are all the time handling this tobacco they make into cigars."

Of the special diseases of these working women, the natural result of the long hours of work, the poor food, the horrible dens in which they live, the Commissioner has much to say. One or two quotations will suffice. "Sewing machine girls are subject to diseases of the womb, and when married mostly have miscarriages. In tobacco factories women are mostly affected with nervous and hysterical complaints, consumption and chest ailments" (p. 171). In his final summary (p. 622) Mr. Peck speaks of the "long hours of labor, the beggarly wages" of these women, and maintains that the facts accumulated by him "furnish the most convincing reason for legislating interference."

As to the number of women thus working. In New York City there are some 20,000. Of 70,000 hands in Connecticut 20,000 are women. These quotations refer more especially to New York City, mainly for the reason that the Commissioner for the State devoted almost the whole of his last report to the condition of the working women of the metropolis. But—as the extracts from the Fall River, Pennsylvania, and Connecticut Reports show—it would be an error to suppose the New York women to be in an altogether exceptional position. Everywhere in America today— save in such occupations as iron-working, e.g., from which women are of necessity excluded—they are forced into direct competition with the men, and are in many cases replacing them. Everywhere we found women forced to work for wages because the husband's were insufficient for even bare subsistence, besides having to tend their children, and go the usual dreary round of endless household drudgery. We have lived in English factory towns and know something of English factory hands; but we may fairly say we have never in the English Manchester seen women so worn out and degraded, such famine in their cheeks, such need and oppression, starving in their eyes, as in the women we saw trudging to their work in the New Hampshire Manchester. What must the children born of such women be?

Before leaving this subject we cannot refrain from referring to an aspect of it that calls for far more detailed investigation than we can give it here. That is, the compulsory prostitution that this state of affairs brings about. A Philadelphia employer of labor quoted in an American newspaper (*The Philadelphia Record*), on the complaint of a girl that she could not live on the wages she was paid, advised her to do as the other girls did, and get a gentleman friend to help her. "Grinding poverty is a very general cause of prostitution, . . . the prominent fact is that a large number of female operatives and domestics earn such small wages that a temporary cessation of business, or being a short time out of situations, is sufficient to reduce them to absolute distress, and it becomes a literal battle for life.... There was a good deal of quasi-prostitution, ... when out of work they cohabit with one or two men, but when work was obtained dropped such associations" (New York, 1886, pp. 187–89). " 'What were the things complained of?' [i.e., in certain mills]. 'Well, I have known of a premium being paid for prostitution in one of the mills in this city.' 'Did you find a case where improper liberties were taken?' 'I have known of bosses trying to compel poor girls to meet them at different places; such were the complaints made to me.... In the Utica steam cotton mills some of the girls were being robbed of their cloth ... while it was found two girls were credited with more cloth than they could possibly have done, and besides they had not half worked; these two girls were not only not respectable, but were bad.' 'And was it known by the employers that they were such?' 'Yes, sir' " (New York, 1885, p. 127). Of the fearful number of women forced to choose between starvation and prostitution in such "flourishing" towns as Kansas City and Indianapolis two clergymen, the Rev. Robert Collier and the Rev. William MacCullough, bore sadly eloquent testimony during our stay there.

THE CHILDREN

They in America, as in England, are gradually ousting the men, where they are not themselves in turn ousted by machinery.

Fall River: "Parents are obliged to do this [send children to the mills] to earn sufficient for the maintenance of their family"

(Cotton Operative, p. 10). "The management has given some of the frames in the spinning room into the charge of boys" (Cotton Operative, p. 152).

New York (1884 and 1886): "Without the wages earned by children parents would be unable to support their families" (Commissioner, p. 112). "To such extremities of want are these people pushed that they are not only compelled to work long and excessive hours, but their children are dragged in, and compelled to work as well" (Commissioner, p. 162).

Kansas: "Two of my boys help me, or I could not keep out of debt" (p. 137) "Children, as a rule, are taken from school when they are of an age to perform any kind of manual labor—say twelve to fourteen years" (Superintendent of lead and zinc mines, p. 142).

New Jersey: "Their [the men's] remuneration because of female and child competition has been reduced to such an extent that only with the aid received from other members of the family are they able to keep the wolf from the door" (p. 265). "Children are occupying the places of adult labor here" (p. 218).

The demand for child labor forces the parents as in this country to lie about the ages of their children, and such laws as exist are constantly evaded or ignored. The workers called as witnesses are almost unanimous in their demand that where laws regulating child labor exist they should be enforced. The opinion of these men and women, even when they are starving parents, are represented by a quotation from the Kansas report: "I think a parent should be compelled to send his child to school until he is fourteen years old. If child labor was abolished it is my opinion that there would be about 35 percent more employment for persons now out of work" (Ironmoulder, p. 110). The opinion of all the Commissioners whose reports we have seen, including even Mr. Flower's, of Wisconsin, is represented by the following words of the New Jersey Commissioner: "There are enough laws in the Statute Book, if properly enforced, at least to restrain the labor of children within reasonable limits, and to make creditable citizens of them, by providing them with a rudimentary education" (p. 266).

But thousands of children are not receiving this rudimentary education. American schools are in all respects admirable, only with the "growth of industry" the power of the children to go to them decreases. When people are starving the children must get bread before they get teaching. In all the Eastern factory towns, in all the lumber districts, even in many a Western city, we heard the same story. "The children must work; they can't go to school." Where the law demands school attendance, the law is evaded. Hence the alarming increase of night schools where young men and women of sixteen and upwards are trying to learn, after a long day's labor, what the law declares they shall learn as little children. In factories the children are "shifted" when the inspectors appear, and thus—unless they are strong enough after ten to twelve hours' work to attend night school—thousands of little ones grow up in complete and dangerous ignorance.

Wisconsin: "Our compulsory education law is inoperative—has been a dead letter since its enactment in 1879" (Commissioner, p. xlii).

Kansas: "Times is so bad that it is a hard thing to send children to school, although schools are so plenty" (Farmer, p. 122). Fall River: "We have a good system of public schools . . . but . . . impracticable for the mill children who attend school only compelled by law" (p. 177). Michigan: "Between the ages of ten and fifteen there were 196,224 children, of whom 30,230 did not attend school . . . over 15 percent."

New Jersey: "Many of them [farming boys] are overworked, and grow up without a chance to get a common school education"

(p. 228). "In 1873 the school census gave 286,444 children between the school ages, of whom 179,443, or 62.6 percent, were enrolled in the public schools, and 69,229, or 24.1 percent, were estimated to have attended no school. In 1882 there were 343,897 school children, of whom 209,526, or only 60.9 attended the public schools, while 89,254 went to no school. In 1878, near the close of the financial crisis, over 62.8 percent of our children attended the public schools, and the average attendance (113,604) was actually larger than that four years later (113,482) although the number of children of school age was nearly 22,000 less" (Commissioner, p. 267).

New York: "According to the last report of the Hon. W. B. Ruggles, State Superintendent of the Department of Public Instruction, we have the following statistics:

Number of children in the State between
five and twenty-one years of age,
meaning the legal school age 1,685,000

Number of children in the common schools 1,041,089

Average daily attendance 583,142

"This means on its face that 644,011 of the children of the State of New York, whose expenses for a common school education are paid by the State, were not found in the schoolrooms during the official year upon which this report is founded. It means that the average daily absence from these schools was 1,101,958." As says another, " 'It is impossible for the mind to contemplate the terrible import of these figures. They are so astounding as to seem almost incredible.' And yet these are the official figures gathered in the same manner for thirty years past" (p. 57). It is true the Superintendent says that in this number there are many being educated in private schools, universities, etc., but the Commissioner points out that "teachers and school officers endeavor to put the best side out," and "unless the State attends to the duty (of enforcing education) it will soon be called upon to provide for these neglected boys and girls in alms-houses, hospitals, asylums, reform schools, and penitentiaries. . . . These remarks," adds the Commissioner, Mr. Charles F. Peck, "are naturally suggested by the statistics, and they ought to be suggestive of our duties as citizens and law-makers." In conclusion, he quotes the summary of the "intelligent officials": "That an army of uneducated and undisciplined children is growing up among us is shown, not only by the State and United States statistics, but by the general observation of men interested in the welfare of children, the widest diffusion of education, and the perpetuity of our free institutions. The terrible fact is further revealed by the incontrovertible evidence of the organization and condition of our schools."

To give some idea of the amount of child labor.

Michigan: "71 establishments in 46 towns and cities . . . representing 26 different classes of business; 292 boys and 62 girls employed from 8 to 14 years old." "In Detroit, 92 different establishments; 287 boys, 85 girls between the ages of 10 to 15" (Commissioner, pp. 238–45). In Connecticut, of the 70,000 hands mentioned above, 5,000 were children under 15. In the cigarmaking trade of New York City 20 to 25 percent of the laborers are children. As to eight different trades child labor is reported as "not coming into competition with adult labor" in two (though in these same trades, cigar-making and telegraphers, a large number of children are employed, to help the adults), and as coming into "direct competition," "crowding out adult labor to some extent," or "the displacing of a man by two boys," in six (p. 74). "And," says the Commissioner, "the testimony as to the employment of 'children of tender age' in tenement houses furnished the evidence of a condition of existing affairs which, I do not hesitate to say, calls for prompt and effective action on the part of the legislature. . . . 'What is the appearance of these child laborers?' 'The physical appearance of the girls in cigar factories is that which we would find in some of the pauper schools that Dickens describes in England, . . . the close confinement in an atmosphere where tobacco is being manufactured is detrimental to full grown people, and must be more so to those not physically developed.' . . . 'Do employees receive a full hour for meal-time during noon?' 'Not over a half an hour.' . . . 'Do they eat their meals in the factory or outside?' 'In the factory; not one in five hundred goes home, for the time allowed is so short.' 'Of what does the meal usually consist?' 'Poor men's sandwich—two pieces of bread, with a little piece of bread in the middle' " (New York Report, 1884, pp. 145–46).

As to hours. Michigan: "In Detroit, 9 hours 50 minutes for the girls and 9 hours 56 minutes for the boys" (Commissioner, pp. 245, 246). In Yorkville, the village of New York mills, 11 hours are the day's work for children under 14. In the cigar factories 95 percent of the children work 10 hours a day. In the smaller bakeries children of from 9 to 13 start work at 11 at night and go on until 4 in the morning. In cotton mills they work from 10 to 11 hours. These instances are taken from States where there is a legal limit, and will give some idea of what happens in other States where there is none of this "annoying legislation."

Their wages. In the 71 establishments in 46 places mentioned above, "the wages were 50 cents per day for the boys, and 31 cents for the girls. The average wages paid to boys in Detroit was 35 cents per day, and to girls 29 cents per day" (Commissioner, pp. 241–45). In New York City, "there are little children working for $2 a week in the large dry goods establishments, . . . and at tailoring, some are employed by the week, when they earn from $1.50 to $2; some work by the piece [at pulling thread out from coats], and the regular price is 2 coats for a cent" (pp. 168–79).

To draw an end with this, we quote a few passages out of many. "There are little children working in the large dry goods establishments. . . . The owners of these large houses in some instances are very severe on the children, and treat them, not like human beings, but like slaves" (New York Report, 1884, p. 168) "I have been in tenement houses and seen children from 7 to 12 years of age at work; . . . when busy they work from 7 o'clock in the morning till 9 and sometimes 10 at night." Louis Troester: "Have seen children working in tenement houses; they were from 8 years of age upwards; they worked from early morning till 9 and 10 o'clock at night preparing tobacco; they were denied the pleasure of going into the streets; . . . and also the privileges of education." Frederick Haller: "You can see any number of children employed in stripping and preparing tobacco; . . . they work from 11 to 13 hours a day—sometimes more; they do not work as long hours as grown persons, but enough to kill them rapidly" (pp. 179, 180). In "cruller bakeries . . . the place is one thorough mass of smoke from the heated oil, . . . and children work all night through, or rather, until 4 o'clock in the morning, . . . and you see children lying upon barrels or about the stores, and they are children from 13 years down to 9 years old" (p. 155). "In the American District Telegraph Company . . . are boys 11 and 12 years of age who are required to be continually at work at least 10 hours a day, running into the worst of places in all sorts of weather, mixing with all kinds of people, into houses of the most damnable disrepute, houses of assignation, and gambling houses; it is very detrimental to their health and morals; they are also compelled to work overtime, and sometimes the hours of their labor commence in the morning, say at 8 o'clock, and they work until 1; and in the evening commence their work again from 6 o'clock until 11 o'clock, and then very frequently work overtime, so . . . while they work 10 hours and often overtime, the hours of their labor extend from 8 in the morning to 11 in the evening; in the 5 hours intervening, may be, frequently compel them to devote an hour or more before they go from their homes to the office, and it cannot be devoted to rest, pleasure, or recreation in the true sense of the term" (p. 155). And in factory towns it is not only the children working in the mills who claim our pity." "Several children," says Col. Wright, in his Fall River Report, "were found supplied with a loaf of bread, which was their dinner, their parents going to the mills in the early morning and not returning until night" (p. 90).

No wonder that the New York Commissioner breaks out: "I plead for the little ones. . . . In these days of legislative interference, when the shield of the State protects the dumb beast from the merciless blows of his driver; when the overworked horse is remembered and released from his work, . . . it would seem pitiable if childhood's want of leisure for rest of body, and education for rest of mind should be denied them. Massachusetts, . . . goes on regardless of consequences, protecting the strong, forgetting the weak and poor . . . under the plea of noninterference with the liberty of the people. The children have rights that the State is bound to respect. Their right is to play and make merry; to be at school, to be players not workers" (p. 355).

To come back from the poetry of this impassioned appeal let us turn finally to the dry facts and figures. New Jersey: "While there were nearly twice as many children employed in the factories in 1880 than in 1870 [for the whole of the United States], the increase in women operatives was 142 percent, while in adult male labor the gain had fallen short of 50 percent" (p. 265). "Must 'Granite Mills' burn down and bury in their ruins the smouldering dust of mother and child before the law will give to them the power of self-protection? Must children plead in vain?"

On the antagonism between the capitalist and the laborer under our present system, and on the internecine struggle between these two, that is the epic of the last part of the nineteenth century, a few final notes. Fall River: "The former feeling of bitterness between the north and south is but an example of the feeling 'twixt employed and employer in Fall River" (Operative, p. 146). "This contest... between labor and capital will continue so long as the purely wage system lasts. It is absurd to say that the interests of capital and labor are identical" (Colonel Wright, Industrial Depression report, 1886). The outcome of this antagonism, and the ending of it, are in the organization of the working classes. This is recognized by all the Commissioners, except Mr. Flower, of Wisconsin.

Pennsylvania: "Capital is concentrated, governed by single intelligence,... labor is diffusive, naturally disorganized... but it is organized labor that the capitalist most fears, and therefore it is with it that he most strongly contends and encourages individual action" (pp. xvi, xvii). Ohio: "The trades having the most powerful and compact organization come the nearest to receiving an equitable share of the joint product of capital and labor" (p. 3). New York: "Organization is absolutely necessary to protect... the wage-worker. There is but one way by which labor can place itself in a position (to sell itself where it pleases), and that is by organization." "This organization is their [the workers'] only strength in contests [with the capitalists] in which sentiment or justice has not yet entered" (pp. 298, 556, 612). The working men themselves almost unanimously declare that in organization lies their hope for the future. "The only way," says a Kansas working man, whose words sum up the opinions of hundreds of his fellows in this and other States, ". . . to advance the cause of labor, is for all to stand together and work as one" (p. 111). Even Mr. Flower, of Wisconsin, has to quote 29 workers out of 37 as favorable to labor organizations, and only 6 are said to be antagonistic to them.

And of the dangerous and bitter spirit of both parties in this contest, one quotation may be taken as typical evidence. "Miners in Ohio have been paraded in some of the press of the State as being in their normal element only when on a strike. . . . Where villainies such as are described above are practices upon a class of men, the wonder is that they have contented themselves with strikes. . . . In many other communities, under similar circumstances, furnishing subjects for first-class funeral would have been resorted to" (Commissioner).

To reduce the possibility of funerals, first-class and otherwise, to a minimum, it is clear that the workers of America must organize. Indeed, they have begun some time ere this to organize, and on the nature of the working-class organizations and their bearing on the future of American politics and economics we shall speak. We end by calling attention to the three chief points as to which, according to the reports, intelligent labor is unanimous: abolition of child labor, eight-hour working day, organization.

7   Organizations— Trade Unions and The Grange*

There are two objects with which a member of the working class may join a labor organization. The two are not necessarily exclusive one of the other. One object is that the individual's position in his particular trade may be more favorable and more secure. The other is that the condition of the working class in general may be improved. Until recently, both in England and in America, the former has been the main, to a large extent the only, idea in the minds of the working men when they joined bodies of organized labor. But, of late years, to this has been added the idea of work for the emancipation of the working class as a whole. This idea is with more and more distinctness shaping itself to that that of the nationalization of all means of production and distribution, and in American more than in England it is taking this form.

Let us quote three different writers in this connection. One is an American clergyman. Writing in the *Century Magazine*, he declares that "Labor is organizing for the purposes of its interests.

---

*The original but misleading title of this chapter was simply "Organizations—The Grange."

It is thus deepening the chasm and intensifying the hostility between the laboring classes and the capitalists. Nearly every trade has now its trade union—some local, some national. These unions are essentially warlike in their aims and in their methods." On the other hand, another writer, equally able, says the Ohio Commissioner, declares trade unions to be simply "a bull movement in the labor market." Finally, the Ohio Commissioner himself holds that "the latter is undoubtedly right, the former wrong, because trade unions, as they exist today, do not recognize any hostility as existing between capital and labor." Our readers will know that, for one, we are on the side of the clergyman in this matter. It is just because the working class is recognizing the inherent hostility between their class and the capitalistic that the second object of trade unions mentioned above is becoming more and more clearly the primary object.

And if we wanted proof of this we could have no better than the words of ex-mayor Grace of New York: "They are organized for defense, not for aggression, . . . their end is to make the working man's life less precarious; to make him a better mechanic, a better man, a better husband and father, and a better citizen." With Mayor Grace the wish is father to the thought. From this optimistic belief the mayor, then getting ready to become ex-mayor, was rudely shaken when in November 1886, he saw organized labor declaring for Henry George as his successor and against Abram Hewitt, and declaring with no bated breath that its opposition to the latter was largely based on the fact that he was a representative of the capitalistic class.

Lastly, we quote from Professor Ely's *Labor Movement in America*, his conception of the meaning and value of working-class organizations. Professor Ely, the English reader must remember, is the political economist of America least unfavorably disposed, or we may even say most favorably disposed, to the laborers as a class. He is the head and front of the Economic Association, and a sore stone of offending to the orthodox school of economists in that country.* According to him, the trade unions and working-class organizations (1) "enable the laborer to withhold his commodity temporarily from the market"; (2) assist the laborer to find the best market for his commodity" (labor, as professor Ely will call it—labor-power as it should be called); (3) "render it easy for the artisan to form useful connections with those pursuing the same trade"; (4) "educate the laborers to prudence in marriage." To many of our readers these "uses" of working-class organizations will appear ludicrously useless, and to yet more they will appear insufficient, by reason of the omission of that one use which to the working class is becoming more paramount—the organization of labor against the capitalistic class, with a view to the ending of the present method of production and distribution.

Against these declarations of Professor Ely and of the Ohio Commissioner, and of the "able writer," we are content to set the declarations and preambles of various working-class organizations to be given in the sequel. It will be found that these are practically unanimous in stating, explicitly or implicitly, that the working-class movement is a political one, and is directed towards the abolition of the present wages-system. And the facts

---

*Professor Richard T. Ely (Johns Hopkins University, later University of Wisconsin) provided one of the earliest positive academic assessments of Marxism in English in his pathbreaking *French and German Socialism in Modern Times* (New York: Harper and Brothers, 1883), pp. 170–88. His study referred to here, *The Labor Movement in America* (New York: Thomas Y. Crowell, 1886), continues to be a valuable source. Also see Benjamin Rader, *The Academic Mind and Reform: The Influence of Richard Ely in American Life* (Lexington: University of Kentucky Press, 1966), and Mark Pittenger, *American Socialists and Evolutionary Thought, 1870–1920* (Madison: University of Wisconsin Press, 1993), pp. 25–42.

of the electoral contests of November 1886, of the various contests since that date, and of the preparations made by the United Labor Party for coming struggles, are yet more eloquent witness on our behalf.

SKETCH OF THE HISTORY OF WORKING-CLASS ORGANIZATIONS IN AMERICA

For the facts now given we are indebted to Professor Ely's book and to the reports of the Bureaux of Labor Statistics. There are "no traces of anything like a modern trades union in the colonial period of American history." But in 1802 the tailors of New York struck for an extra $4 a month, and marching about the city with a band, compelled their fellows to come out on strike, until the clapping of their leader into prison, ended this first working-class effort in America.

Between 1800 and 1825 sporadic appearances of unions of one trade in one place occur. They are illustrated by the New York Society of Journeymen Shipwrights, incorporated April 3, 1803; the New York House Carpenters' Union, 1806; the New York Typographical Society, 1817; Albany Typographical Society, 1821; and, at last, the movement quitting New York State, the Columbian Charitable Society of Shipwrights and Caulkers of Boston and Charlestown, 1822.

From 1825 the working-class movement really begins. More local unions appear; unions between workers in different trades and in one place, unions between workers of the same trade in many places, finally between workers in different trades and in different places, are gradually evolved. Boston and New York are the chief centers of the work from 1825 to 1861. But in 1830 a working man's convention met in Syracuse, New York State, and nominated a governor for the State. In the same year, the workmen's party of New York helping, the Democrats elected three or four members of the legislature. In 1833 the General Trades Union of the City of New York, prototype of the Central Labor Union, to be presently described, met, and in 1835 there is mention of a National Trades Union. The ten years before the Civil War are remarkable for the number of trade unions organized on a national basis. A list of these follows: Instrumental Typographical Union, 1850, 28,000 members, July 1856; National Trade Association of Hat Finishers, 1854, divided in 1868 into two organizations, the one retaining the old name, 3,392 members, the other calling itself the Silk and Fur Hat Finishers' Trade Association, 643 members; the Sons of Vulcan, 1858; the Iron Moulders' Union of North America, 1859; the Machinists and Blacksmiths Union of North America, 1859.

The years 1861 to 1886 are yet more full of the movements of labor. The Civil War had, after the fashion of the Crusades in the history books, stirred the minds of men, brought different types into contact, even if into collision, opened up avenues of communication, and above all, forced the attention of men on labor problems by the sudden and unrighteous encroachments of businessmen and, if we may be allowed the pleonasm, adventurers. In 1863 the Brotherhood of the Footboard, an organization of engine-drivers, was founded, and a year later it became the Grand International Brotherhood of Locomotive Engineers. In 1865, still another year later, one of the most important bodies in the world, the Cigar Makers' National Union, started. In 1867 it was International. An International Union of Bricklayers and Masons, in 1865; the Order of Railway Conductors (originally known as the Conductors Brotherhood), in 1868; the Wool Hat Finishers'

Association, in 1869; the Trade Union of Furniture Workers (later the International Furniture Workers Union), in 1873; the Brotherhood of Locomotive Firemen, in 1875; the Amalgamated Association of Iron and Steel Workers, made up of the Sons of Vulcan, the Associated Brotherhood of Iron and Steel Heaters, and the Iron and Steel Roll Hands' Union, in 1876; the Granite Cutters' National Union of the United States, America, in 1877; Brotherhood of Carpenters and Joiners of America, in 1881; Cigar Makers' Progressive Union of America, 1882; the National Hat Makers, in 1883; the Railroad Brakemen, in 1884; the Coal Miners' National Federation, in 1885; the Journeymen Bakers' National Union, in 1886—these are the chief trades unions formed since the war.

"Other trades unions which must be mentioned are the following: The Chicago Seamen's Union, the United Order of Carpenters and Joiners, the Plasterers' National Union, the Journeymen Tailors' National Union of the United States, Deutsch Amerikanische Typographia (composed of those setting type for German books or periodicals), American Flint Glass Workers, and the Universal Federation of Window Glass Workers. Working men who have national or international organizations of which I am not acquainted with the precise names are the boiler makers, stationary engineers, metal workers, piano makers, plumbers, railroad switchmen, shoe lasters, spinners, streotypers, telegraphers, silk weavers, wood carvers" (Ely, pp. 65, 66). The membership of the American Trades Unions varies from 2,000 to 25,000 each, while there are also many thousand Americans who belong to the English Amalgamated Engineers, Amalgamated Society of Carpenters and Joiners, the machinists, millwrights, smiths, and pattern makers.

THE GRANGE

Before turning our attention to the genuine working-class organizations, a few words on the Grange or the Patrons of Husbandry. This body, with its unfortunate name-word "patrons," is an essentially class organization, and not a working-class one. It is composed of farmers, and farmers only. Number 6 of its Declaration of Purposes reads: "Ours being peculiarly a farmers' institution, we cannot admit all to our ranks."

The Grange is local, is state, is national in its character. It professes to advance the interests of all, apparently by the self-satisfactory method of advancing those of the one. The one is, of course, the agricultural constituency, as the patrons put it; the employing fraction only of this, as facts show.

Started in 1866, on the initiative of P. H. Kelly, a Minnesota farmer, who had been sent south just after the war by the Agricultural Department of the Government, the Grange went through the usual stages of a successful organization—struggle, growth, political temptation, reaction, recovery. In 1886 Maine added 1,100 "patrons" and 11 new granges; the corresponding number for New Hampshire and Pennsylvania were respectively 700 and 9; 1,700 and 18; Massachusetts increased its membership 100 percent, with 10 new granges; Connecticut, 150 percent, with 16 new granges.

The objects of the Grange are very definite, as far as the actual farming interest is concerned, and are vagueness itself as far as it relates to the people generally. To make farms self-sustaining, to diversify crops, to discountenance the credit and the mortgage system, to dispense with a surplus of middle men, to oppose the tyranny of monopolies, are definite aims. But there is an air of vagueness about laboring for the good of mankind, developing a better manhood, fostering mutual understanding, suppressing prejudices.

The Grange is not a political organization. Upon this point it is very explicit and reitatory. It claims to be educational and cooperative, and has many cooperative associations (132 in Texas alone), banks, insurance companies, and so forth. Yet by its agitation this organization has helped to secure the passing of the Interstate Commerce Law, the Oleomargarine Law, and other enactments.

Recognizing the antagonism between capital and labor today (Declaration 4), yet the Grange makes no definite contribution to the solution of the problem of their reconciliation. Not that the organization ignores economic questions, as witness the resolution passed at the annual session of the National Grange in 1885: "Resolved that the Worthy Lecturer of the National Grange be instructed to continue the distribution of subjects for discussion quarterly, to subordinate granges, and that questions of political economy be given prominence," etc. On further investigation the questions of political economy resolve themselves into "gold, silver, greenbacks, national banks, corporations, interstate and transcontinental transportation, and the tariff as it relates to agriculture."

From the above it will be seen that at present the Grange is a trade union only in the narrow sense; is an organization of farmers alone; is not a political body. It may in time become leavened with the leaven of the general working-class movement; but as it is at present constituted the Grange is probably more likely to be a hindrance to that general movement than a help.

We pass to the chief organizations—the Knights of Labor, the Central Labor Unions, the Socialistic Labor Party, and the United Labor Party. These are organizations of organizations, and as such hold the same position in respect to the bodies they group together as a generalization of generalizations holds to the inductions that it summarizes.

8 | Knights of Labor— Central Labor Unions— Socialistic Labor Party— United Labor Party

The Knights of Labor Organization is so well known on both sides of the Atlantic that all that is really necessary here is the definite statement of certain facts, dates, and figures, and an attempt to make plain the exact position of the K. of L. at the present time. On Thanksgiving Day, 1869, Uriah S. Stephens, a tailor of Philadelphia, called together eight friends. The nine (is one not irresistibly reminded of the theory that a tailor is one-ninth of a man?) founded the K. of L. At first a secret order, whose very name was not known to the public, and whose cabalistic five stars were for long an example of *omne ignotum pro terrifico* to the Philadelphians, thus became in June 1878 an organization, public at least as far as its name and its general objects are concerned.

Roughly speaking, the scattered unions of the various towns of the various states and the scattered units of labor have affiliated themselves with the Knights, and thus formed another one, and the largest, of the national labor organizations. Each local society is called the Local Assembly (LA). Its members may be of one, or more than one, trade. Three-fourths of the members of a new LA must be wage-workers. Anyone but a banker, stockbroker, gambler (with cards), lawyer, and alcoholic money-maker may be admitted. Local Assemblies are grouped into DAs (District Assemblies). These are either geographical or technical. LAs and DAs, alike represented by numbers, are grouped up as a whole into the General Assembly, or delegate body representing the whole order. The first General Assembly was held in 1878; membership, 80,000. A General Assembly has taken place in each year since that date. Membership in 1883, 52,000; 1884, 71,000; 1885, 111,000. The membership, as estimated by Professor Ely, for 1886, would be 300,000 to 500,000, though our friend Colonel Hinton, who knows much of the internal working of the order, estimates its numbers as at least a million.

What are the principles of the K. of L.? Here at once it becomes necessary to distinguish the principles of the organization from those of its members. This necessity arises from the fact that the majority of those who join the organization and subscribe to its principles understand neither the aim of the former nor the meaning of the latter. Both of these last are in the main socialistic. It is impossible here to analyze the four paragraphs of the preamble or the twenty-two declarations that follow them. To one or two points only can we call attention. The burden of the four preliminary paragraphs is that capitalists and corporations (companies) need checking; that the industrial masses need organization; and though the K. of L. are formed "not as a political party,... most of the objects herein set forth can only be obtained by legislation." With the contradiction contained in these last two quotations we are the less concerned, as the movement of November 1886 and the action of thousands of the Knights in regard to it are the best comment on the two phrases and the best endorsement of the latter of them.

One only of the twenty-two "aims" can we note. But this is in truth the sum of all of them. It is number 19. "To establish cooperative institutions, such as will tend to supersede the wage system, by the introduction of an industrial cooperative system." Now this is pure and unadulterated Socialism.

Briefly: scientific Socialism teaches that the basis of our society today is the method of the production and distribution of commodities; that the misery and inequality in that society are due to that method; that the essence of that method is unpaid labor. Cooperative institutions are to be established—i.e., cooperation both in production and in distribution. That this is the true reading is shown, practically, by the extensive establishment founded by the K. of L. for the production of commodities (mines) and their distribution (stores). Now a cooperative system, or, as the Knights at times put it, a universal cooperative system, that is "to supersede the wage system," is not possible unless the means of production and distribution are systematized and are universal. Universal cooperation in production and distribution is impossible without the universal possession of the means of production and distribution—i.e., without the abolition of private property in these.

But the real significance of all this lies in the fact that in the Knights of Labor we have the first spontaneous expression by the American working people of their consciousness of themselves as a class. This expression—this organization—at first almost unconscious, are becoming every day more conscious. Necessarily confused at first, the very confusion of the movement is evidence of its spontaneity and its reality. At present there is much uncertainty as to leaders, or even as to the direction in which movement is to be made. But all this is sorting itself, and it will not be long before the American working class will be organized, and moving with definite purpose towards a definite end.

The Knights, then, are a huge heterogeneous organization; and whilst certain of its members are conscious and avowed Socialists, and others are unconscious Socialists, the mass know no more of the teachings of Socialism than they do of their own supposed principles.

As a consequence of this and of other causes, there are two clearly defined parties within the organization, into one or the other of which all the minority of earnest men is entering. The one party, led by Mr. [Terence V.] Powderly, the Grand Master Workman, is conservative, reactionary, and must go back yet more completely to the capitalistic side as the intensity of the struggle increases. The other party is advanced, socialistic, and must launch out into Socialism open and avowed. The split between these parties will probably turn on the two questions of political action and the open declaration of Socialism. But whatever form it takes, such a split is, we think, imminent.

Already there are among the rank and file plentiful signs of dissatisfaction with the action of their leaders. The vacillating, temporizing conduct of these last in respect to the strike of the Chicago packers in the autumn of 1886, to the subsequent railroad strikes, to the longshore strike and others, above all their disapproval, in direct contravention of the principles of the order, of the eight-hour movement of May 1886, have made many of the Knights believe that it is not only the interest of the working class that is in the minds of their chiefs. More than mere rumors have been rife of the subordination of these to the interests of the capitalists and of the Roman Catholic Church. A great many delegates who went up to the convention of 1886 at Richmond with the profoundest belief in Powderly came away with that belief shaken or shattered.

A comparative study of the position of the Knights in the eastern and western towns still further bears witness to this general fact. In the former, where the mass of the members are more in contact with, and more under the influence of, the bosses of the movement, two things are more noticeable than in the western towns further removed from their reactionary influence. First, the organization is much less really effective for good to the working classes, and shows much more signs of being under capitalist pressure; second, its relations to other labor organizations are much less harmonious in the eastern towns.

CENTRAL LABOR UNIONS

This name may be used generally for a number of bodies all of the same nature, but with names so varying as General Trades Unions, Trade and Labor Assemblies, Trade and Labor Councils, Federations of Labor. They are certain central bodies organized with a view to the men and women of a particular district working together. These Central Labor Unions are more hopeful organizations than even the Knights. They are, in the first place, more avowedly socialistic; and, in the second, more avowedly political organizations. The declarations of principles of the New York and of the Kansas City CLU, for example, are definite and decisive, without any of the vagueness that runs through the preamble and principles of the Knights. They speak out plainly against the wages system, on the ground that it is based on unpaid labor, and recognize the necessity and inevitableness of a complete change of that system. Here again, as with the Knights, the mass of the members, unfortunately, do not understand the full meaning of the ideas to which they subscribe.

The Central Labor Unions do not hesitate to work at present for certain means towards the ultimate end, and they do this as a political party altogether apart from the old parties. A brief quotation from the Kansas City CLU, sent us by one of its chief organizers, J. H. Trautwein, may be taken as generally typical of the Unions. "We, the undersigned, believing all the old parties have failed to legislate for the people at large, and have betrayed the trust reposed in them by the masses, and only enacted measures that result in creating paupers and millionaires, pledge ourselves to sever all affiliations with all the old parties whatever, and sign the following club roll for the purpose of forming a party of the industrial masses." Then follow certain measures to be worked for, many of which—such as the prohibition of child labor, equal wages for women and men, an eight-hour working day—are endorsed by the Knights also.

The difference between the CLU and the K. of L.—a difference at present distinctly in favor of the former—is due to the different historical development of the two bodies. The Unions are the result of many years of evolution in Labor organizations; and upon them has been brought to bear the practical experience especially of the German Socialists. The Knights, as we have already shown, were the first spontaneous and indigenous outgrowth of the American working class as it became conscious of itself.

THE SOCIALISTIC LABOR PARTY*

This party, founded originally by the Germans, now numbers many thousands of members of all nationalities in America. The

---

* The original name of this organization, founded in 1876, was the Workingmen's Party of the United States, whose first year of existence is informatively discussed at length in Philip S. Foner, *The Workingmen's Party of the United States: A History of the First Marxist Party in the Americas* (Minneapolis: MEP Publications, 1984). At the end of 1877, the organization of about 7,000 members split into two separate organiza-

men of its earlier days—F. A. Sorge and others—are beginning to reap at last their deserved reward. This organization, with its German, American, and Scandinavian branches throughout the States differs from all others in certain important points. (1) Long before any of the others the Socialists understood that there was a labor question, and understood what that question really was. Thus they have been, unconsciously to their scholars in many cases, the teachers of the working classes. (2) They state clearly that society is made up of only two classes—"that of the workers and that of the great bosses." (3) They formulate clearly their demands that the land, the instruments of production (machines, factories, etc.) and the products of labor become the property of the whole people. (4) They announce sufficiently their means: "to realize our demands we strive to gain control of the political

---

tions over the question of whether or not electoral activity or trade-union organizing should be prioritized. One of the new groups (led by some associates of Marx such as Friedrich Sorge, and such trade unionists as Adolph Strasser and Samuel Gompers) called itself the International Labor Union, which went out of existence by 1884, many of its members merging into the Federated Organization of Trades and Labor Unions, which reorganized itself with other forces as the American Federation of Labor in 1886. The other organization, in the words of Henry Kuhn (who was a central leader from 1890 to 1906), was called "the 'Sozialistische Arbeiter Partei,' a name somewhat woodenly translated into English as 'Socialistic Labor Party,'" with "that terminal 'ic' " being dropped by 1890 (Henry Kuhn and Olive Johnson, *Socialist Labor Party, 1890–1930* [Brooklyn: New York Labor News, 1969], p. 13). Another split—again over electoral policy—resulted in the formation of the International Working People's Association discussed in the next chapter. The SLP was still able to attract some critical minds and alert activists in the period when Marx and Aveling wrote about it, although it suffered from sectarian and factional disabilities (as they note). Later, from 1890 until his death in 1914, the dominant personality in the SLP was Daniel DeLeon, discussed in a capable biography by Stephen Coleman, *Daniel DeLeon* (Manchester [UK]: Manchester University Press, 1990). The best single study of the SLP is by two veteran members who left the organization: Frank Girard and Ben Perry, *The Socialist Labor Party 1876–1991: A Short History* (Philadelphia: Livra Books, 1991).

power with all proper means." (5) They are in alliance with the Socialistic Labor Party of Europe.*

What are the relations of the Socialistic Labor Party to the other organizations of America? In the first place, the vast majority of its members are also members of one or more of these organizations; and only a few, not understanding the position of the movement in America, hold aloof from the Knights or Central Labor Unions. As a consequence, these other organizations are becoming, to a constantly increasing extent, infiltrated with Socialism, and slowly their vague, indefinite aspirations and ideas are becoming formulated in terms of that science. With this the individual Knights and Unionists are being gradually brought over, not only to the understanding of Socialism, but to open declarations of themselves as Socialists and as members of the SLP.

The complete bringing about of these desirable results is delayed by two things chiefly. One is the distrust of Socialism held until recently by the average American working men—a distrust born of his ignorance of its principles, its aims, its methods. Most K. of L., for example, protest strongly against being called Socialists. The other impediment lies in some of the German Socialists themselves. A few of these, as already hinted, not understanding the movement generally, and still less understanding it in America, are anxious to "boss the show" in that country. As long as that is possible, the movement in America will not be American. Socialism, to be effective there, must be of native growth, even if the seeds are brought from other countries.

That is, whilst the Germans will in the future, as in the past, direct the thoughts of their fellow workers, and suggest ideas to them, they will have to be content after a time to stand aside, and

---

*That is, the various socialist and labor parties that in 1889 formed the Socialist International, also known as the Second International.

let the so-called leadership of the movement pass into the hands of the English-speaking peoples. The most clear-headed Germans in America quite see this. Their work has been, is, and still will be, to teach and to initiate organization. But already their American brethren, under their tuition, are organizing for themselves on the basis of Socialism. From the moment this is the case, the policy and duty of the Germans are to withdraw into the background, and whilst never relaxing in energy, or ceasing to inspire from within, to let the forefront of the movement be American.

THE UNITED LABOR PARTY

Out of these labor organizations, but especially out of the last one considered, i.e., the Socialistic, has grown the United Labor Party. The date of birth of this was the elections in November 1886. Then, for the first time, the class consciousness of the working people became embodied in a definite political movement of antagonism to the capitalist class. The startling success of the Labor Party in New York, Chicago, Milwaukee, and other places, taught their opponents, and taught themselves, something of the extraordinary power and significance of this new force in politics. Both of the old parties, Democrat and Republican, are frightened at the working-class movement. They will do all they can to get the Labor Party on their side. In this they will ultimately fail. Weaklings, especially at the outset, will succumb to the temptation; but the United Labor Party of America has, to use an Americanism, "come to stay," and to outstay all others.

The Henry George movement in New York, though often called Socialistic, did not, strictly speaking, deserve that name. The chief interest and importance of it were, as in the case of the Knights of

Labor, in its spontaneity and Americanness. The Socialists played their usual part here. As *The Communist Manifesto* has it, they, the vanguard of the working classes, cast in their lot with any genuine working-class movement. Their teaching for years before, and their action at the time, had, of course, much to do with originating and shaping the November movement; and the leading organizers, writers, and speakers were, in most cases, Socialists by avowal or in heart. Of course with these were associated many men and women who would by no means have accepted the name of Socialists as applicable to themselves.

In such towns, as Chicago, Milwaukee, etc., further afield than New York, the running of working-class candidates in November 1886 was on somewhat different lines from the mayorality contest in which George figured. In certain cases, at least, the men working in these contests in the more outlying districts understood more clearly than the New Yorkers the real questions at issue, and the real principles upon which the working class is and must be in conflict with the capitalists.

After the November (1886) elections the Labor Party began getting itself into yet more definite shape; and at a meeting held on January 13, 1887 in New York, a permanent organization, a platform, and a constitution for the United Labor Party of America were agreed upon. In these there were, from our point of view, certain weak points in detail. But the party as then constituted condemned the present industrial system, and recognized that the "ultimate emancipation of labor can only be attained by the abolition of private ownership in the productive forces of nature." Here, then, we have, for the first time in America, the working class organized as a distinct political party, opposed alike to Democrat and Republican, taking its stand on the nationalization of the productive forces of nature.

This basis is not sufficiently broad nor sufficiently firm. Nationalization of the land is all that Mr. George and his followers mean; and already (September 1887) they have parted company with the men that see further and more clearly than themselves. At the Syracuse Convention in August 1887, the Socialists, by very questionable means, were practically expelled for the time being from the United Labor Party. But the Socialists can bide their time, and probably the time will not be long. A political party that repudiates the nationalization of all the means of production and distribution, and only hankers after the nationalizing of the land, is assuredly not a Labor party.

The most significant fact, none the less, is the formation of a party bearing even the name of Labor. Its preliminary bossing by half-hearted men and professional politicians was an inevitable incident in its evolution; as inevitable as its ultimately becoming a purely Socialistic organization.

The example of the American working men will be followed before long on the European side of the Atlantic. An English or, if you will, a British Labor Party will be formed, foe alike to Liberal and Conservative; its ultimate standpoint will be Socialistic, although, like the American Labor Party, it may have to pass through several preliminary stages; and its ultimate fate, like that of its transatlantic prototype, will be the attainment of supreme political, and then of supreme economic power.

9 | The Cowboys*

The cowboys of the West have been this long-time objects of interest to Americans of the other points of the compass, and recent events have made the English public familiar with them under certain aspects. But there is one aspect under which this class of men seem little known to their fellow-countrymen, and are almost wholly unknown to other peoples—that is, in their capacity as proletarians.

To most people, until lately, the cowboy was a "bold, bad man," as reckless of the lives of others as of his own, with vague ideas as to morals, and especially as to the rights of property; generally full of whiskey, and always handy with a revolver. If the spectators of the "shows" in which he has been exhibited on both sides of the

---

*One of the charms of the Marx-Aveling discussion of the U.S. working class is this first-ever Marxist analysis of cowboys in the Old West. For recent scholarship in this and related matters, in the spirit of the present chapter, see: Patricia Nelson Limerick, *The Legacy of Conquest: The Unbroken Past of the American West* (New York: W.W. Norton, 1988); Patricia Nelson Limerick, ed., *Trails: Toward a New Western History* (Lawrence: University of Kansas, 1991); and Richard White, *"It's Your Misfortune and None of My Own": A History of the American West* (Norman: University of Oklahoma Press, 1991).

Atlantic have modified their ideas upon this human subject, the modification has been, as a rule, in the direction of a recognition of the fact that he is not much worse or better morally than his more civilized fellows, and in his manners, as in his physique, he is for the most part considerably the superior of these.

In the present chapter we desire to show the reader that which the cowboys themselves have made plain to us, that they are distinctly members of the nonpossessing and yet producing and distributing class, that they are as much at the mercy of the capitalists as a New or Old England cotton-operative, that their supposed "freedom" is not more of a reality than his. Further, evidence will be given that the cowboys, as a class, are beginning to recognize these facts, are becoming anxious that the general public should know them, and, best of all, are desirous, through the medium of either the Knights of Labor, or some other working-class organization, to connect themselves with the mass of the laboring class and with the general movement of that class against the tyranny of their employers.

Our first acquaintance with these facts was made at Cincinnati, and in a sufficiently odd way. Some delightful German-American friends, in their anxiety to show us all the sights of the city, had lured us into a dime museum. The chief attraction at this show, pending the arrival of Sir Roger Tichborne, who came the next week, was a group of cowboys. They were sitting in twos and threes in various little raised platforms, clad in their picturesque garb, and looking terribly bored. Presently, a spruce gentleman, in ordinary, commonplace garments, began to make stereotyped speeches about them in a voice metallic enough for stereotyping. But, at one platform, he mercifully stopped short, and told us that Mr. John Sullivan, alias Broncho John, would take up the parable.

Thereupon, a cowboy of singularly handsome face and figure,

with the frankest of blue eyes, rose and spoke a piece. To our great astonishment he plunged at one into a denunciation of capitalists in general and of the ranch-owners in particular. We were struck both by the manner and the matter of this man's talk. It had the first and second and third qualifications for oratorical success— earnestness. Broncho John evidently knew what he was talking about, and felt what he said. The gist of his speech is embodied in the last paragraph but one. To that need only be added John's appeal to the newspapers of the East that they should do what the Western ones were afraid or unwilling to do, and state clearly the case of the cowboys, their complaints, and their demands.

As Broncho John invited any interested in the question to communicate with him, we answered his invitation, and on the following day had a long talk privately with him. The main points of the many we learned from him through the medium of that conversation, and of a little pamphlet he gave us, will now be noted.

There are some 8,000 to 10,000 cowboys (this is Broncho John's estimate, and is considerably below the actual number), and "no class is harder worked, ... none so poorly paid for their services." The reason why they are so poorly paid and hard worked is simple enough: "They have no organization back of them," while their employers have "one of the strongest and most systematic and, at the same time, despotic unions that was ever formed to awe and dictate to labor." ... The conditions under which the cowboys work are such that organization is immensely difficult, in many cases well-nigh impossible. They are dispersed over miles upon miles of huge plains and desolate wastes, a few here and a few there, so that concerted action seems almost out of the question. Yet so many are, it appears, "awakened to the necessity of having a league of their own" that a Cowboy Assembly of the K. of L. or a Cowboy Union is sure to be started in the near future. Meanwhile, the fact that such a league is desired by the cowboys is significant enough, and even more significant is their employers' fear of any such combination. One means by which the bosses hope to ward it off is by issuing orders that the men "must not read books or newspapers." Small wonder the cowboys regard such an "order" as "tyrannical in the extreme." A pathetic example of the belief of the cowboys in a movement of some sort we found in Broncho John's conviction that a return of Blaine (as president) would mean that "all the thieving would go on," while the election of Henry George would "make a change."

As to the actual work and wages of the cowboy. The work is necessarily extremely arduous and dangerous. For some six to eight months in the year—i.e., the working time on the plains—he has not only to be in the saddle from morn to night, but often the whole night through as well. To look after these huge Western herds of cattle, to keep a cool head during stampedes and "milling" is not small matter. "I have been with a party," says John Sullivan, "when we were obliged to ride 200 miles before we got the cattle under, . . . in all that time not one of us took a moment's rest or a bit to eat." In getting the cattle across streams milling often occurs, i.e., the beasts take fright and swim round and round and in every direction but that of the shore. As a consequence "many a good cowboy has been drowned," and it is not "uncommon for a party to spend three weeks or a month in getting a herd of 4,000 cattle across a stream." Further, there are the innumerable dangers from bands of marauders, Indians, and prairie fires to face; and, into the bargain, the herd must not only be delivered safe and all told, but they must have increased in weight since leaving the ranch. "The rule is, the cowboy must fatten the cattle on the trail, *no matter how thin he may grow himself.*"

And for such work as this the ranchers, who expect their

employees to risk their very lives in looking after the stock, pay the best paid of the cowboys—$25 a month. Moreover, the cowboy has himself to find his outfit, except his horses, which belong to the ranchers, and a cowboy's outfit is a heavy item of expense. He must have a heavy fur hat, Mexican "chafferals" (leggings), a "slicker" (oilskin coat), a good saddle, a "quirt" (a heavy whip some three feet long), spurs, revolver, specially made boots, etc., etc. In all, this costs him about $145. But the cowboys who cannot afford such an outlay at the start are supplied by the ranchers, and supplied with goods of a kind that barely last through a season. For these the rancher charges $15 a month out of the wages; so inferior is the outfit, that it has constantly to be renewed, and thus the cowboy remains constantly in debt.

From climactic and other conditions it is well-nigh impossible for cowboys to obtain any employment during the "off-time," and these men must therefore keep themselves and their families on the $120 to $150 dollars that can be earned in the year. Nor is this the only difficulty with which the cowboys have to contend. Black-listing is apparently not peculiar to the East of America. It seems to flourish even in the Wild West, and the cowboy is as much its victim as the cotton-operative. "It may easily be seen then," says Broncho John, "that the cowboys have a serious struggle against actual want, and such is the system of the Ranchers' Society they dare not protest. Experience has taught them that to ask for an increase in wages means immediate discharge from the service. But that is not the worst. The moment a man is discharged by any member of the Ranchers' Society his name is sent to every other member, the name is turned to in the books of each ranch and a black mark placed opposite it. This is called 'black-listing' the cowboy. He might as well leave the country at once."

But perhaps the greatest injustice, the most flagrant piece of robbery, perpetrated by these large ranch owners, and one which affects both settlers and cowboys, is that of "repleving" cattle. To "repleve" is wild-western for seizing all unbranded cattle, and of late the right to do this has been claimed by the Association of Ranchers under the Maverick Law. A settler or cowboy gets a few head of cattle; in time these increase, and a few years ago he could sell them to the Association or other traders at "fair market price." But this did not suit the ranchers. Just as they—to use Broncho John's words—are "grinding out" the settlers from the land which they have opened up; just as the "road agent" is ousting the settler from the little homestead he has raised, so the ranchers want all the cattle—and take it. Any unbranded animal is claimed by them. Against this iniquitous proceeding two men—settlers we believe—named Cooper and Leineberger, tried to protest. They refused to give up the cattle that was their property. Hereupon the Association (The Wyoming Stock Growers) instituted an action against them (in 1884) for infringement of the Maverick Law. The defendants' counsel pleaded as a demurrer that while the law was in force in that State, it was against the Constitution of the United States. Judge Parks would give no decision at all, and Judge Corn gave his decision in favor of the Association. Thereupon Cooper and Leineberger appealed to the Supreme Court, with what result we have been, so far, unable to learn. For such cases as this never get into Eastern papers, and the Western ones mostly fear to touch them. The process, like everything else, is under the terrorist regime of the ranchers. Meantime, "repleving" goes on merrily, and the small settlers, robbed of their little stock, become cowboys and the wage-slaves of the ranchers, who are all staunch upholders of the sacred rights of property.

10 | **Anarchists***

It is necessary, in the first place, to make clear our own relations to Anarchism, and the relations between Anarchism and Socialism.

It is hardly necessary to say that, as Socialists, we are not Anarchists, and are, of necessity, entirely opposed to the methods and aims of Anarchism. It is true both Anarchists and Socialists attack the present capitalist system. But the Anarchist attacks it from the individualist, conservative, reactionary point of view, the Socialist from the communist, progressive, revolutionary standpoint. The two "schools"—if the one can be called a school which has no definite program, no clear teaching—have, in fact,

---

*General points made at the beginning of this chapter were elaborated when Eleanor Marx presented the work by George Plekhanov (spelled Plechanoff when she translated it for English-language readers in 1895): see *Anarchism and Socialism* (Chicago: Charles H. Kerr Co., 1906). For a more sympathetic assessment, see Daniel Guerin, *Anarchism* (New York: Monthly Review Press, 1970). On the other hand, see Hal Draper, *Karl Marx's Theory of Revolution, Volume IV: Critique of Other Socialisms* (New York: Monthly Review Press, 1990), pp. 107–75, 270–304

For further discussion of the so-called anarchists of Chicago dealt with in this chapter, see Editor's Note at the end of this chapter.

nothing in common. It is characteristic that the most violent attacks made on us during our tour in 1886 were made by Anarchist writers and speakers. The Chicago capitalist press wanted us to be hanged after we had landed; Herr Most's paper, *Die Freiheit*, was for shooting us "on sight" before we landed.

This personal fact is mentioned because it is characteristic of the general Anarchist tactics. In every country, wherever a revolutionary movement has begun, a small handful of men has cropped up (as often as not thoroughly honest, but usually led or urged on by police agents), calling themselves Anarchists, yet very vague and contradictory as to what they mean by this name. Everywhere they have proved a hindrance to the real working-class movement; everywhere they have proved a danger, since the police have egged them on to premature and disastrous *emeutes* [disturbances]; happily, they disappear when once the movement attains real power and meaning. In a word, where the working class has come to years of discretion, and where from a vague feeling of misery and unrest it has grown to understand its true position, has awakened to class consciousness, Anarchism dies out. Anarchism ruined the International movement; it threw back the Spanish, Italian, and French movements for many years; it has proved a hindrance in America; and so much or so little of it as exists in England is found by the Revolutionary Socialist party a decided nuisance. Everywhere Anarchism (especially when police inspired) talks very big; but while there is "great talk of revolution, there is great chance of despotism." The Socialist believes in organization; he believes in political action, in the seizure of political power by the working class as the only means of attaining that complete economic emancipation which is the final aim. As to what the Anarchists believe, it is a little difficult to say, as no two give the same definition of their views. But the tree is known by its fruit; and the fruit of Anarchism has invariably been reaction, a throwing back of the movement, and a confusing of men's minds.

But while it is true that Anarchism has proved, to some extent, a hindrance in America, chiefly because so many Americans have been induced to call Socialism Anarchism as a mere protest, or from want of accurate knowledge, the power of Anarchism, pure and simple, must not be overestimated. There is a great deal of sound and fury, but it signifies nothing. In their very stronghold, Chicago, events have taught them the folly of their own doctrines; and at the November election, in 1886, there were no heartier workers for the Labor candidates than the Anarchists, who until that time had seized every opportunity of denouncing the political action of the Socialists. Moreover, it must be borne in mind that well-nigh every word spoken by the chief defendants at the Chicago trial, of which more in a moment, could be endorsed by Socialists; for they preached, not Anarchism, but Socialism. Indeed, he that will compare the fine speech by Parsons in 1886 with that of [Wilhelm] Liebknecht at the high treason trial at Leipzig will find the two practically identical.

Our very antagonism to the Anarchist doctrines, therefore, made it the more incumbent upon us, whilst in America in 1886, to do all in our power toward demanding for the Chicago Anarchists that justice which was denied them. It was our duty, and we made it our business, to speak at every meeting we held in America in favor of a new trial for the condemned Anarchists of Chicago. And this on the following grounds:

(1) The trial took place too near the events of May 4, 1886, in point of time.

(2) The trial took place too near the events of May 4, 1886 in point of place. A change of venue was necessary for justice. This

is recognized in the case of the police when held on a charge of murder. Thus a private detective agency man, Joy, arrested in November of the same year on a charge of shooting one Begley, in an unarmed and peaceful crowd, was not tried where the event occurred.

(3) The arrests were made without any legal warrant. This statement is true, not only of the eight men sentenced, but many others, who were thus illegally arrested, kept in prison four months, and then discharged without even being brought to trial.

(4) The houses, offices, and desks of the accused were broken into, and their contents taken by the police without any search-warrants having been issued.

(5) During the trial and after its close the police made, at judicious intervals, opportune discoveries of bombs and the like in Chicago. These discoveries were simultaneous with any awakening of public feeling on behalf of the accused. Thus, four infernal machines were discovered a month after their arrest, and the attempt was actually made to use this discovery as evidence against the imprisoned men. In the opinion of many people these bombs found by the police were also hidden by the police.

(6) The jury was, at least in part, made up of men prejudiced against the accused. Amongst the many whom the prisoners' advocates challenged was one who admitted that he had formed a distinct affirmative opinion as to their guilt before the trial began, and who was certain that no amount of evidence could shake that opinion. Judge Gary overruled the objection to this man, and he served on the jury. Besides this one special case, there was general evidence that the jury was packed. We quote from the *Chicago Inter-Ocean* of October 2, 1886. The application to Judge Gary for a new trial was made on October 1. "The affidavit of E. V. Stevens, a travelling salesman, . . . states that the affiant is well acquainted

with Otis S. Favor; that he knows the latter to be intimate with Ryce had said to him in his presence and the presence of others, while Ryce was engaged in summoning jurors, the following words: 'I am managing this case, and know what I am about. These fellows are going to be hung as certain as death. I am calling such men as the defendants will have to challenge and to waste their challenges.' The defendants' counsel then said that Favor had refused to appear in the court to testify openly or to do so by affidavit, unless he was compelled to do so by order of the Court. They therefore asked that the Court order a subpoena to compel Favor's appearance.... Judge Gary: 'I shall overrule the motion.'"

(7) The judge was unfair. Two cases have already been given. He ruled out of order questions as to whether the police had given money to the witnesses for the prosecution. He ruled in order the introduction of translated extracts from a work of Most's, although there was no evidence that any of the accused had ever seen the book, and although it was known that two of them (Parsons and Fielden) could not read the language in which the book was written. To the counsel for the defense, when they pleaded against the introduction of such evidence as this, Judge Gary said, "Sit down, and don't make scenes." He allowed the bloody clothing of the policemen that were killed to be introduced in court. When, on Captain Black protesting, State-Attorney Grinnell said, "I could bring in the shattered corpses of the policemen," Judge Gary uttered no reproof. He overruled an objection to evidence as to conversations between prisoners and the police. To the defendants' counsel, cross-examining, he said, "I think you ask much too much." When the verdict and sentence where given by the jury, unimpeachable witnesses state that the judge went out to his wife, who was waiting for the result, and said, "All is well, mother. Seven to be hanged, and one fifteen years. All is well."

(8) The counsel for the prosecution, Mr. Grinnell, was passionate and venomous. In his opening speech he denounced the accused as "godless foreigners." When the group "Freiheit" was mentioned, the familiar German word had to be translated to Mr. Grinnell, whose comment was, "Oh yes, freedom to send people into the air!" He tried hard to use the after discovery of infernal machines (v.s.) as evidence against the accused men. When the desk, stolen and broken into by the police without a warrant, was found to be fitted by a key in the possession of Spies, the demand was made that the keys should be returned to their owner. "Oh, he'll never need them again!" said Grinnell.

(9) The witnesses upon whose evidence the men were condemned were tainted. Wilhelm Seliger, who turned States' evidence, had been living in the police-station, admitted many conversations with the police, and the receipt of money from them, and was contradicted on essential points by witnesses equally independent of prosecution and defense. Of Gottfried Waller, the second States' evidence witness, the same assertion may be made. The most important witness, one Gillmer, who saw everything—saw Schnaubelt (never in custody) throw the bomb, saw Spies light it, saw Fischer with them—was a semitramp, out of work, living in the prison, who said nothing of all he saw at the inquest nor for days after. He knew all details of build and face of men in the alley, but not a word of the speeches. Shea and Jansen, two detectives, the latter of whom had been in the Anarchist organization with other policemen for sixteen months, and a number of newspaper reporters, for the most part on intimate terms with the police, completed the list of the witnesses for the prosecution. Shea confessed that he tried to get Spies to sign an incriminating paper in prison, without letting him see its contents. Jansen attended secret meetings, and furnished the police with notes of

them. When anything was wanted to egg the Anarchists to action, he considerately provided it. One Malcolm MacThomson heard a compromising conversation between Spies and Schwab, in which "pistols" and "police" were mentioned, and the question, "Will one be enough?" asked. He confessed that he did not understand a word of German, and it was proved that Spies and Schwab always spoke in German to one another.

Against these may be set their own contradiction, and the evidence of an army of independent witnesses. These show that the Haymarket meeting was peaceful and orderly, that many women were present, that no incendiary speeches were made. Thus, a certain Freeman saw Parsons, Fielden, and Spies, not in the alley à la Gillmer, but on the wagon; heard Parsons suggest adjournment as it was raining; heard Fielden say, "I am ready. Wait a minute, then we'll go." This witness contradicted the police evidence. Dr. James Taylor, aged seventy-six, was in the alley at the time the bomb was thrown from a point twenty feet from the alley. He testified to the perfectly peaceful character of the meeting until the police arrived.

But especially Mayor Harrison must be quoted. Was present at the meeting until within twenty minutes of explosion. Had agreed with Chief of Police that it must be dissolved if not peaceful. Tone of speeches generally such that feared a point might be reached when he must dissolve it, as he was determined to do so soon as any use of force was threatened. Parsons' speech a political tirade. Witness told Captain Bonfield (Chief of Police) it had been a very tame speech. Went to police-station, told Bonfield there would be no trouble, and it would be better if his men went home. Then left, thinking all was well.

(10) The American press to some extent, the Chicago papers to a considerable, and the *Times* and especially the *Tribune* of that

city to a hideous extent, clamored for the hanging of these men. Anything more indecent, undignified, and panic-striken than the *Chicago Tribune*'s articles we have never, in a fairly large and varied experience of journalism, seen. If these men are ultimately hanged, it will be the *Chicago Tribune* that has done it. And as proof that the condemned were condemned not because the evidence showed they were murderers, but because it showed they were Anarchists, one quotation from the *Tribune* will suffice: "Chicago hangs Anarchists." There are no words of qualification: "Chicago hangs Anarchists."

During the months of September to December 1886 a change was wrought in popular feeling. The speaking and writing of many men and women, altogether opposed to Anarchist teachings, the constant appeal to the sense of justice of the American people, the gradual recovery of the latter from the state of unreasoning fear into which the events of May and the infamous newspaper articles had worked them—these and other things had their effect. By the time of the municipal elections in November a great body of public opinion had declared for a new trial. Then came the thunderbolt of the success of the Labor Party at the elections. From that moment it was certain the men would not be hanged on December 3. On Thanksgiving Day (November 25) Captain Black, the magnificent advocate for the Chicago Anarchists, obtained a stay of execution.

In April 1887 we received from our friend, Captain Black, the printed copies of his brief and argument, and of his oral argument before the Supreme Court of Illinois on March 18. In his accompanying letter, dated April 6, he writes: "Let me as a lawyer say to you that I deem it [the argument] unanswerable, and I know it had not been met, although upon the other side they filed printed arguments aggregating over 546 pages. . . . I think the opposition really expect a reversal of the judgment; and for myself I am absolutely confident of the result." The opinion of the better class of journals was in the main the same. And the opinion of almost every one, when the first angry panic was over and calmer judgment prevailed, was, even as far back as December 1886, that unless some new and much more reliable and conclusive evidence could be brought forward by the police at the second trial, no jury would convict the Chicago Anarchists of murder.

Of one thing there can be no doubt. After our Ulysses' wanderings and the coming into contact with Knights of Labor, Central Labor Unionists, and so forth, in many towns, we can say with confidence that the vast majority of the working class were of opinion that a miscarriage of justice had occurred. Of course this majority were not Anarchists. Nor were they even Socialists. To the teachings—the avowed teachings—of the eight men sentenced they were as intensely opposed as any Socialist could be. But they considered that justice had not been done.

The present position of affairs in this celebrated case is (September 19, 1887) that the Supreme Court of Illinois has refused the application for a new trial, and has confirmed the sentence, fixing as the date of execution, November 11. Probably appeal will be made to the Supreme Court of the United States. It seems impossible that men can be done to death on such no-evidence as was brought against the Chicago Anarchists, and if they are executed we have no hesitation in declaring that the American people will be guilty of a cowardly and brutal murder.

We have thought it wise to retain in this volume that which we wrote originally in May 1887, as throwing light upon subsequent events in connection with the Chicago Anarchists, and as having a general bearing upon trials in a capitalistic society of men whose greatest crime is antagonism to that society.

✕ ✕ ✕

Editor's Note: It is hardly the case that the so-called Chicago anarchists were followers of Pierre-Joseph Proudhon, Mikhail Bakunin, or any other anarchist luminary. In fact, they were much closer to the orientation of Karl Marx—rejecting the benign view of the capitalist state and electoralist orientation that were relatively common among some members of the Socialist Labor Party (who in some cases happened to be influenced by the more statist orientation of Marx's sometime-ally/sometime-opponent Ferdinand Lassalle). Friedrich A. Sorge saw the martyred Chicago activists as outstanding working-class organizers: "It is undeniably the meritorious accomplishment of the Chicago anarchists to have brought into this marvelous mixture of workers of all nationalities and languages a certain order, to have created affinity, and to have given the movement at that time unity and goals." He believed that this particular variant of "anarchism began in Chicago, stemming from the misguided policies of the Socialist Labor Party's executive. Once started on this precipitous path, the excited and easily excitable workers of Chicago could not be restrained anymore." In 1883 they joined with other forces—including some like Johann Most who were influenced by anarchist perspectives—to form the International Working Peoples Association at a conference in Pittsburgh. Sorge quotes one of the Haymarket defendants:

> If you take time to glance through the pamphlets written by Spies ... and look at the explanation which he gives of socialism and anarchism, then you will see that his socialism hardly differs from that of the Social Democrats and that there anarchism appears as the ethical side of socialism. It can also be

not unknown to you from whom or which writer he takes his thoughts about socialism [i.e., Karl Marx and Frederick Engels]. One time the Pittsburgh program with which many were unsatisfied was discussed. Spies explained: "The Pittsburgh program is secondary, our program is the *Communist Manifesto!*" And indeed the first large meeting which was held had as its basis the *Communist Manifesto*. Spies had Parsons, Gorsuch and other Americans round him in the office of the *Arbeiter-Zeitung* on whom he impressed the major teachings from the booklet.

Sorge concluded that the leadership of the Chicago anarchists and the Chicago workers were one and the same, a group of "intelligent and energetic people. The Germans, August Spies and Michael Schwab, the American Albert Parsons, the Englishman Samuel Fielden, supported by many others, were active and untiring agitators and the first three also served as writers and editors of the *Arbeiter-Zeitung* and *Alarm*. To the aforementioned characteristics must be added great courage, loyalty of conviction, and untouchable personal honor. Friend and foe alike still think of them today as men of character." Sorge, *Labor Movement in the United States* (Westport, Conn.: Greenwood Press, 1977), pp. 210–12.

In contrast to all of this, see Frederic Trautmann's sympathetic biography of someone closer to Bakunin-influenced anarchism, *The Voice of Terror: A Biography of Johann Most* (Westport, Conn.: Greenwood Press, 1980), plus Sam Dolgoff, ed., *Bakunin on Anarchy* (New York: Vintage Books, 1972). It would appear that perhaps three of the Haymarket martyrs—Adolph Fischer, Louis Lingg, and George Engel—had a greater affinity to this more classically anarchist current in the International

Working People's Association, although Engel probably expressed the view of all in stating that "anarchism and socialism are as much alike, in my opinion, as one egg to another," adding his view that the primary difference involved a tactical question on how to achieve a socialist society: "I say: Believe no more in the ballot, and use all other means at your command." This comment can be found in the valuable source edited by Dave Roediger and Franklin Rosemont, *The Haymarket Scrapbook* (Chicago: Charles H. Kerr, 1986), p. 44.

11 | Some Working-Class Leaders

We bring this series of notes on the American phase of the working-class movement to a close with a short account of some of the people whom we met in the States. This account will include brief reminiscences of Henry George, the Sinaloa folk, certain of the Woman Suffrage advocates, Messrs. Hinton, Schevitch, Black, Morgan, Vrooman.

HENRY GEORGE

To English readers it is not necessary to give any description of George or of his views.* It is far more important to show how he

---

*Less well known today, Henry George authored a best-seller on political economy, *Progress and Poverty* (1879), and had considerable influence in the United States and Europe in radical and labor circles. His book argued that land belonged to society, which created its value, and that poverty could be eliminated if land were properly taxed through what he called "the Single Tax." A sympathetic portrait can be found in Anna Angela George DeMille, *Henry George, Citizen of the World* (Chapel Hill: University of North Carolina Press, 1950). Also see Arthur N. Young, *The Single Tax Movement in the United States* (Princeton: Princeton University Press, 1916).

and they have been modified by the movement that forced them both to the front in November 1886. We met Henry George late in September (the 29). He was already nominated for Mayor of New York, and the election was due on November 2, whilst we were leaving New York on October 2 for eleven weeks of agitation tour. At such a time, under such circumstances, he and ourselves holding our respective position, it will be understood that our talk was on momentous matters, and, for the greater freedom on either side, was understood at the outset to be a private conversation. As since that day we have had no opportunity of again meeting Henry George, our notes upon him and his utterances must be understood as limited to opinions and expressions, to whose publication we have reason to believe he would have and could have no objection.

Henry George is a little man, with exceedingly clear blue eyes that seem exceedingly honest, a straight-cut mouth, red beard, and bald head. In manner he is sharp, quick but not abrupt, and outspoken. He believes—his books are expressive of his creed—that the land question is at the bottom of everything. Solve that, he seems to think, and the evils of society will lessen and vanish. He does not, like the Socialist, regard the mode of the production and distribution of commodities, with its private property in the means (of which land is but one) of that production and distribution, as the basis of modern society, and therefore of the ills of that organization. And he does not see how, from our point of view, this idea of his is especially untenable in America—the country to which the capitalist method came ready-made, and where it now exists in its most brutal and uncompromising form—the country in which, at the same time, there is the largest area of land as yet unclaimed or uncultivated, and the country in which, probably, peasant proprietorship will hold out longest.

But from this, as we think, economic error in regard to the basis of our present system and the necessity of attacking the land question first, it must not be imagined that Henry George recognizes no other evils than those connected with the holding of land tenure. His answer, dated August 26, 1886, to the Conference of Labor Associations, when they asked him if he would stand for Mayor, is evidence of this point. Here are one to two quotations thence. "Those general conditions which, despite the fact that labor is the producer of all wealth, make the term working man synonymous with poor man. . . . The party that shall do for the question of industrial slavery what the Republican party did for the question of chattel slavery must . . . be a working-man's party. . . . I have seen the promise of the coming of such a party in the growing discontent of Labor with unjust social conditions. . . . The wrongs of our social system. . . . There is and there can be an idle class only where there is a disinherited class."

In these quotations there is something more than condemnation of the land system. "General conditions," "industrial slavery," "unjust social conditions," "the wrongs of our social system," are the terms used. Clearly, Henry George recognizes that society is wrong, and nowhere in this letter does he refer to the land as the basis of this wrong. Indeed, the word "land" never once occurs in the letter. Unfortunately, clear as is George's recognition of the rottenness of our social, i.e., our capitalist system, he does not anywhere in this document state clearly what he believes to be the root of this rottenness. Only in one passage does he give even a hint at this. "The foundation of our system is in our local governments." It is in these "local governments" that our capitalist or commercial system appears in its most concentrated, immediate, and concrete form.

As to the immediate remedy, Henry George, not unnaturally

as the potential candidate for the mayorship of New York, is more definite. This is political action. "I have long believed that the Labor movement could accomplish little until carried into politics," and "the increasing disposition to pass beyond the field of trades associations into the larger sphere of political action," are two phrases from the letter already utilized.

Now, whilst as to the immediate remedy the opinions just quoted of George became confirmed more and more strongly as the electoral contest went on, his opinions as to the actual cause of the "unjust social conditions" also took more definite shape. Brought into close and constant contact with the men and women that were the life of the movement in New York by his name, men and women who were, as we have said, really Socialists, this man, a drop of spray on the momentary crest of the vast and gathering wave of an immense popular movement, was consciously or unconsciously forced into ever clearer and more clear declarations as to the private ownership of the means of production and distribution. These declarations are to be found throughout his speeches during September and October, and in his open letters to Abram Hewitt, the capitalist candidate; and their number and definiteness increased as the time for the Mayorality election drew near.* We have not space to quote all of these—and to quote only a part of them would be of little value; but from them and from the result of the contest on November 2, and from the course of events since, we venture upon a prophecy as to the political future of Henry George. Like the Knights of Labor, he will come to the parting of the ways, one of which goes onwards and the other backwards. How near he even now is to

---

*Actually, there were two capitalist candidates in this election—the Democrat Hewitt, who narrowly won the election, and a young Republican Party hopeful named Theodore Roosevelt, who came in third.

that trenchant point he, better than all other men, should know. Paradoxical as it may seem, he possibly does not know better than all other men what his decision will be. But the decision will have to be made. Will he go forward with the labor party resolved on nationalization, not of land alone, but of raw material, machinery, means of credit, capital, or fall back towards the ranks of the old parties and be absorbed of them?

The question is answered by the events of the Syracuse Convention, and by Mr. George himself, in his own paper, the *Standard*. Henry George declared against Socialism in the *Standard* of August 6, 1887, in a series of articles betraying the most astounding ignorance of that against which he declared. By doing this he took the sea-end of the two steps which we said he must take, and took beyond all power of retracing. As far as a real working-class movement is concerned, he is a ruined man.

THE SINLOA FOLK

These are a company of men and women who have obtained possession of the State of Sinloa in Mexico, call themselves the Credit Foncier Company, have planned and built a city, and propose living therein as a sort of Zoar among the cities of the plain. The Chairman is Albert K. Owen, who is no relation or connection of Robert Owen; the Treasurer, John W. Lovell; the Attorney, Lewis H. Hawkins; the Secretary, Davitt D. Chidester; the Representative in Mexico City, Ignacio Pombo. Departments of Deposits, Surveying, Law, Motors, Police, Transportation, Diversification, Education, Farming, Pharmacy, each have a head. Amongst these "heads" are Edward and Marie Howland, two of our earliest visitors in America, and two of those who left on us the deepest impression of sincerity and earnestness. The intention is to form another of the "communities" of which America has already seen not a few, with a combination of the communistic life within and the capitalist life without. Such a combination is, as it seems to us, but one more of those attempts at a compromise between the antisocial system of today and the social system of tomorrow that are foredoomed by their intrinsic nature.*

This, then, is an attempt of the Fourier and Saint-Simon order, and will probably meet with the same fate as is encountered by all undertakings of this kind. The establishing of small islands of more or less incomplete communism in the midst of the present sea of capitalist method of living, only ends in the overwhelming of the islands by the sea. The necessary smallness of the scale upon which such an experiment must be made handicaps its success. It is true that the whole scheme of the Sinaloa community is on broader and longer lines than, perhaps, any other that has yet been started. Yet, the riddle of modern society is not likely to be solved in this way. The success of an experiment of the kind, assuming that it is attained, would be an encouragement, possibly even an example, to the workers. But probably the final solution of the riddle will be by the conquering of political power in every country by the proletarian party, by their subsequent conquest of economic power, and by the abolition of private property in the means of production and distribution, leading to a communistic society commensurate with the whole of the nation. Let it be added, nevertheless, that if earnestness of purpose, integrity, high sense of honor and of the beauty of life could insure success in

---

*Classic surveys of such communities can be found in John Humphrey Noyes, *History of American Socialisms* (New York: Dover Publications, 1966) and Charles Nordhoff, *The Communistic Societies of the United States: From Personal Visit and Observation* (New York: Dover Publications, 1966), which first appeared in 1870 and 1875 respectively.

such an undertaking, that of the Sinaloa community, judging from the members of it with whom we came into personal relations, is assured.

WOMAN SUFFRAGISTS

It was at the house of the Treasurer of the Sinaloa community, John Lovell, that we met Henry George, and also one of the representative Woman-Suffrage women of America, Mrs. Devereux Blake. With another of these, Isabella Beecher Hooker, sister of the late Henry Ward Beecher and of Mrs. Harriet Beecher Stowe, we spent perhaps the most happy and assuredly the most peaceful hours of our stay in America. A word or two may be said here upon our experience of the American women who are in the front of the battle for the extension of the suffrage to their sex.

They appear to be like and yet unlike their English sisters laboring in the same field. They are like them in their nonunderstanding of the fact that the woman question is one of economics and not of mere sentiment. The present position of women rests, as everything else in our complex modern society rests, upon an economic basis. The woman question is one of the organization of society as a whole. American female woman-suffragists are like the English in the fact that they are, as a rule, well-to-do. And they are like them in that they make no suggestion for change that is outside the limits of the society of today.

But the American woman-suffragists differ from the English in one very important particular. They are ready and willing to listen to the ideas of other schools of thought whose shibboleth is not identical with theirs. They are beginning to understand that this special question is only part of a much larger one. They are beginning to understand that it can only be answered satisfactorily and completely when the great economic problem is solved. The two women mentioned, and others of the same school as they, eagerly listened to any attempt at a statement as to the method of solution of that problem, and were ready to engage in the more far-reaching struggle for the emancipation of the workers as well as that for the emancipation of their own sex. And in this wider view of the contest for liberty there is of course no narrowing of the view as to the woman question especially; nor does any one lose the womanlike in the larger mind.

Another difference between American and English "advanced" women is that the former are much more outspoken. They call things honestly by their names, and are not like the English, afraid of being thought "improper." When the *Pall Mall Gazette* and Mr. Stead were dealing with certain questions that assuredly concern women at least as much as they concern men, a very plain-speaking letter on the subject was drawn up, and a number of well-known "advanced" women in England were all aflame to sign it at first. But the fear of that member of their sex whose name is Grundy came upon them, and they nearly all with one accord began to make excuse. Not that they had altered their opinions; they were only afraid to make them public. Among the advanced women in America such cowardice as this would be impossible.

COLONEL RICHARD J. HINTON

A New York visitor, earlier even than the Howland husband and wife, and a man as sincere and earnest as they. English born and Chartist bred, Hinton came over to America on the right side of things political, and has been upon it and in the forefront of it ever since. He was all through the Civil War, and took out from Boston the first corps of newspaper fighters and writers for the North. He was close friend of Ossawatomie Brown—John Brown, as the English knew him—and there were almost as many and as large offers made for his head as were made for that of his friend. Since the war ended Hinton has worked at journalism; and when the Labor Bureaus were started, he held, and still holds, official positions under them. But he as never ceased to fight as well as to write. Since the battle for the Negro slaves was won, he has been engaged in that on behalf of the wage slaves. Always active with pen and with tongue in any movement, small or large, for the greater freedom of any class, he has never lost sight of that largest of all movements that is destined to swallow up all others, as Aaron's rod the magicians'. No man or woman in America is more clear than he as to the bearing of all the various struggles here and there, now and then, upon the one great struggle between the working class and the possessing. And, whatever form that struggle assumes during the many years that we hope, for man's sake, Hinton may live, it is certain that he will be in the thick of it, and that his energy, enthusiasm, and bravery will be of incalculable value. Equally certain is it that his wife, a beautiful-faced, beautiful-natured Irish woman, will be by his side, strengthening him and their cause.

SERGIUS SCHEVITCH

A cosmopolitan of the cosmopolitans. Russian by birth, this remarkable man speaks and writes perfectly German, French, English, and American, and, for aught we know, half a dozen other languages. He can conduct a newpaper and address a meeting in one of five tongues, counting American and English as two. He not only speaks and writes American—he thinks it. He has as clear an understanding of the conditions of society in the States, of the political situation there, of the position of the working-class movement, as Hinton himself; and this intimate knowledge of the land of his present adoption is accompanied by a knowledge not less intimate of the general European movement and its details in different countries. For a long time Schevitch was editor of the *New Yorker Volkszeitung*, the most important German labor paper in America. This post he only resigned to take that of editor of *The Leader*, a journal started just before the November elections of 1886 on behalf of Henry George in his candidature for the mayorship of New York. After the elections the paper was continued as an organ of the working classes, and both Hinton and Schevitch held postions on it, the latter still at the head of affairs. Physically, Schevith is as remarkable as he is mentally. He is of magnificent physique, and very handsome face; his voice is singularly strong and sweet. His wife, an actress of considerable power, was Helena von Rackovitz, the heroine of the duel that ended in the death of Ferdinand Lassalle, and the heroine of George Meredith's *Tragic Comedians*, a book whose indebtedness to Helena von Racovitz' own Memoirs has been hardly sufficiently acknowledged by its distinguished author.

CAPTAIN WILLIAM BLACK

Another physical and mental giant, but this time pure American. His name has gone out into all the earth as the advocate for the Chicago Anarchists, and to him, more than to all the rest of the world put together perhaps, they owed the long remission of their sentence, and will owe any commutation of it, should that communtation ultimately come. It was in their prison that one of us first met Black. On the one side of the iron grating in Cook County Jail were eight men, seven under sentence of death and one penal servitude for fifteen years. On our side were a few men-visitors and two women. One of the latter was Mrs. Neebe, wife of the eighth prisoner. She is dead since. The other was Mrs. Black, a bright, energetic, fresh little woman. She and her husband scarcely every missed paying at least once in the day a visit to the men, either at 9:30 A.M. or at 4 P.M. The presence of both of them, even when they were not talking to one of the prisoners or intertwining a little finger with one of theirs through the grating (the only shaking hands possible), must have been a great solace. Her cheerful courage and enthusiastic faith in the ultimate getting of justice done were, without a doubt, of much help to the condemned men. But even more helpful, if possible, must have been the presence of her husband. It was easy to pick him out from among those present. Fully six feet in height, and built in perfect proportions, with long, quite white hair, a darker moustache and imperial, and very strong, keen eyes, such as only the kings and queens among men have.

Only a few hours later he and his indomitable little wife were with us, and during our four days' stay in Chicago hardly one went by without a visit from them although, according to Mrs. Black's statement, her husband was anything but a "calling" man. Fortunately for us the five or ten minutes of his average stay anywhere became hours with us and hours among the most memorable of all that made up our American time. We found the wife bitten with the most amiable variety of Anarchism that attacks those by whom neither the history nor the economics of the question has been studied, and who, seeing men unjustly treated because they are called by a particular name, straightway label themselves in the same fashion. But the husband was quite "sound." He defended his clients as men unfairly treated. He was in full accord with their Socialist speeches at the trial, but not with the Anarchist ones ascribed to them before it. He fully recognized the need for an education, an organization, a political program, as well as the not less necessary agitation; and so, for the matter of that, did his wife.

Nothing was more interesting than to see how in Black the enthusiast and the practical man were blended and yet distinct. He would discuss the future of the working-class movement with a contagious fire; the next moment, if you asked him a question as to the Chicago trial and the appeals he was then prosecuting, he was the calm, contained judicial lawyer, upon whose purely legal opinion you could depend as confidently as upon his unswerving fidelity to any cause in which he believed.

Black also had been through the war, and his tales of that time of trial were as delightful as the *Arabian Nights*. And most delightul of all was the singing of the "Battle Hymn of the Republic" by our two friends. Many a time he had sung it on the march, when his men passed the word up to him for a song; and he sang it in our hotel rooms with a swing and a ring in his voice as if he were marching along at the head of a company. If only some Chicago "drummer" (Anglice, commercial traveller) had looked into our room at 10 o'clock that November morning and seen Black thundering out the Battle Song of the North, his wife singing "seconds," two other people listening, and, I think, four with tears in their eyes, what a quartet of asses he would have thought us!

WILLIAM MORGAN*

Another Chicago friend, a working man in the stock sense of the word, and a very typical example of the best type. A Birmingham artisan orginally, this man is physically a curious antithesis to Black. He is considerably below middle height, and the generally stunted growth that generations of artisan heredity often produce; but mentally he ranks with Hinton and Black in our remembrance. An open and avowed Socialist and a thoroughly dependable man, he never disguised his opinions, never denied his principles, never truckled to man or to party. Yet he held a good postion in some railway works, we fancy; and such was his influence among his fellow-workmen that on more than one occasion they had, upon his advice, abandoned a useless strike, whilst on other he had conducted similar movements to a successful issue. To Morgan, more than to any one else singly was due the excellent organization of the working-class movement in Chicago that realized 25,000 votes in November 1886, and frightened the Democrats and Republicans into an alliance, offensive and defensive, against the new third party. And Morgan's courage is not less than his integrity. He kept his head cool and clear all through the time of terror after the bomb-throwing and police-killing in May 1886, by degrees got others round him, cool and clear-headed, and with their help stayed the unreasoning panic. And when we held the public meeting in Chicago that, according to the *Chicago Tribune* and *Times*, was to be proclaimed beforehand and then broken up by the police, with "threatenings and slaughter" as to arrests and imprisonment and hanging for all the principals, it was Morgan who took the chair.

---

*Aveling and Marx may have mis-remembered Morgan's first name. The most prominent Chicago socialist fitting their description was Thomas J. Morgan.

But, when we write thus of this one earnest, single-souled, faithful worker for Socialism, we remember that he himself would be the first to point out that there are scores and hundreds like him in America. It is impossible now to recall every one of the number of thorough men and women, with true hearts and shrewd heads, in the movement, whom we met in every town we visited; but some of the names, for our own satisfaction, we should like to place on record. Only it must be remembered that just such another list—and a much longer one—might be made of men and women, as earnest and reliable, had we space and our readers' patience. In Chicago Morgan has, besides other helpers, Warner and Kruger; way out West in Kansas City are Tesek and Ruf (cigar makers, who make their own men Socialists); and Trautwien ("ein ganz gewohnlicher Schneider"); in Cincinnati, Walster (editor of the *Zeitung*), Borckhauser, and Fritz; in Springfield, Mass., Mielliez, Mache, Nagler; in its namesake Ohio, the Hruzas, man and wife; Brown of Boston; Mueller of St. Paul's; and the trio, Nymanover, Evers, Blumenberg, at Minneapolis; Harris in Brooklyn; Seiler and Bushe the Bridgeport and New Haven coworkers; Winter of St. Louis; Nicolai of Louisville; Paul of Davenport; Eberding of Bloomington; Dorn of Baltimore; Grahamer of Williamsport; Osborne Ward and Heidemann of Washington; and the Blatz family of Milwaukee. Many names, especially those of working men, we omit in memory of the black list.

We should like to describe in full one whose name is given in this fragment of a list. But trying to make anybody who had not known Otto Walster understand what manner of man this rare soul is, needs a George Meredith at least, if not a Heine or a Balzac, or these two last in one. There are two aspects of the poetry of a movement like that of Socialism. The one is furnished by the genuine proletariat, by their sufferings, their awakening, their feeling after hope, their aspiration, their understanding, their resolve, and their victory, and of this song only the earlier verses are as yet sung confusedly. The clear voice of these, and yet more, the full clarion of battle and the paean of triumph are not yet sounded.

But the other apsect of the poetry of the working-class movement is already more definite and distinct in form. It is yielded by the artistic souls that, today, are making for the promised land beyond, and mark the way thither by their singing. Of such as these is Walster. Poet, dramatist, novelist, an artist to his soul's core, he descends into the common ways of men so that he may help to lead men from them. He makes the path out of the desert at once plainer and more smooth. He goes along it apparently carelessly, with a sort of devil-may-care swing; but he misses no flower that may be noted by the way; nay, he plants many himself, and for the less favored souls gladdens all the journey with an eternal geniality and with flashes of an exquisite and pathetic humor.

When he was not at work on his paper, he was slouching about with his hands plunged far down into the outer pockets of his long great-coat, and his slouch hat on the back of his head, devouring chestnuts, showing us everything, and commenting on all that he showed with infinite wit, unforced, unobtrusive. He took us to panoramas, to dime museums, to saloons, to *cafes chantants*, to theaters. Was it not at one of these last that his attention was distracted from the stage by a lady and gentlemen before us, of whom the representative of the ungentler sex had the largest and most projecting ears ever fastened on to human head? They were like the sales of a windmill; and Walster watched them through most of one act. Then, still regarding them stonily, he said, as if to himself, "Und sie liebt ihn!"*

---

*"And she loved him!"

THE VROOMAN BOYS

Let us end with a description more within compass than that of Walster, and whose objects are of not less moment in the American movement. The youthfulness of many of the working-class agitators and writers is, in so young a country, very much in keeping. At Cincinnati two boys came to see us, and said, quite as a matter of course, that they were the editors of an American labor paper in that city. But the most interesting instance of this juvenility in work was in Kansas City. We were speaking at a private meeting on Sunday night there, before the public one on the Tuesday, from which over five hundred people were turned away at the door, and at which forty new members of the American section of the Socialist Labor Party were enrolled. A very young and eager face on the left stood out from all others at the preliminary private meeting. Later on, we were introduced to its owner, Walter Vrooman, the boy-orator. He was then only seventeen, but was well known as a public speaker on labor questions, and an immensely popular one. He had been "run in" several times for open air speeches, and on one occasion the police had to let him out of the jail by the back way, or the crowd, angry at his arrest, would have had him out by the front or burned the prison down. Yet the lad's head was by no means turned by all this, as one little thing showed significantly. On the Tuesday night, when our speaking was done, the crammed and jammed audience of something getting on for 2,000 people shouted for the boy, he rose and spoke two sentences only in about twice as many seconds.

Walter and his brother Harry were the editors of the American labor paper of Kansas City, *The Labor Inquirer*. Harry, nineteen years of age, had contributed to the Bureau of Labor for Kansas State a most valuable set of facts and statistics on the Labor movement. Both boys we found frank, open-hearted, delightful; quite boys still and with a keen sense of fun, as their elder brother, a Unitarian clergymen, and not yet a Socialist, found out, for they chaffed him good-humoredly, but mercilessly. A fourth boy, fifteen years of age, they announced as "coming on," and sure to work with them before long. Walter has, since our visit, gone to New York and created a huge sensation there by his really wonderful speaking, while more recently Harry has also gone East upon the warpath. Probably we shall hear them in England one of these days.

Such a phenomenon as the Vrooman boys would be impossible in any other country than America. But its occurrence there, as well as the various nationalities of the names we have given in these pages—e.g., Black, Morgan, Mielliez, Macdonald, McGuire, Hruza, Trautwein, Vrooman—show the universality of the Socialist movement in America, and tell of the certainty of its ultimate triumph.

12 | Appendix

The reader will have noted that thus far this volume is a reprint of the work written by us in 1887, and published in 1888, and that the "Reports" quoted by us are none of them later than the year 1886. Apart from the fact that, in any case, the volume of 1888 is at any rate a document of some historical significance, the condition of the Working Class in America, and the relative positions of Labor and Capital are in this year, 1890, the same as they were when we wrote—"only more so."

In most instances, the Labor Bureaux Reports from which we quote are still the latest on the particular subject of which they treat, as the different States generally take up some special subject for each year. Thus the Commissioners for Washington deal in the first volume with "Industrial Depression," in their second with "Convict Labor," and in their third with "Strikes and Lock-Outs." And so, for the most part, the Reports quoted are still the latest American contributions to the general question.

As proof of our statement that things today are much as they were when we wrote, a few quotations will be given from some of the Labor Bureaux Reports received by us since the publication of *The Working-Class Movement in America* in 1888. We can quote but a small portion of the invaluable statistics before us, and, as in our earlier quotations, we have chosen what is characteristic and common rather than what is sensational or exceptional. Besides the Official Reports, we would call the attention of readers to the admirable articles of Mrs. Helen Campbell, Mrs. Florence [Kelley] Wichnewetzsky, and the two articles by Mr. Shearman, published in the *Star*.

Child-labor—a horror undreamed of by the Seers who had Visions of Hell, but not of modern bourgeois society—is the main "note" of our capitalist world. Men are gradually being replaced by the "cheap" labor of women, and both men and women are being replaced by the still "cheaper" labor of little children. And so in a land of such go-a-head capitalism as America, we should logically expect to find child-labor at its worst. And we do. America has, perhaps, the best schools in the world, but the children of the working class are being rapidly and surely drawn away from the schools into the Factories, Workshops, "Domestic Industries" (read Sweating Dens). Everywhere child-labor in the States is on the increase, and this, despite all the warnings, the appeals, the eloquent denunciations of the Factory Inspector and Bureau Commissioner.*

In chapter 6 of this volume we quoted chiefly on this subject from the admirable Reports from New Jersey and New York. Let us see what these and other States have to say on the matter in their most recent volumes.

---

*Among later studies on child labor—a topic which still seems to await its own full-scale history—are John Spargo's 1906 classic *The Bitter Cry of the Children* (New York: Quadrangle Books, 1968) and Katherine D. Lumpkin and Dorothy Douglas, *Child Workers in America* (New York: A.M. McBride, 1937). For more current realities in today's global economy, see United Nations, *Exploitation of Child Labor* (New York: United Nations, 1983), and Alec Fife, *Child Labour* (Cambridge: Blackwell, 1991).

At the Seventh Annual Convention of Commissioners, Mr. Lee Meriwether, of the Missouri Bureau, said: "Regarding the inspection of Factories, how is it possible to ascertain whether or not children under the legal age are working, when both the manufacturer and the parents of the children agree in declaring that the child is of legal age? In questioning the parents as to the age of their children working in factories, I have sometimes had them laughingly ask, 'Do you mean their real age or their factory age?' Their factory age is generally anywhere from one to three years more than their real age" (*Michigan Report*, pp. 325). "The worsted yarn mills (Philadelphia) employ very young girls, sometimes violating the law against child labor" (*Working Women in Large Cities*, Washington, 1889, p. 23). "In whole industries ... few girls were found who had received much education" (Ibid., p. 25). From "the summary of age at beginning work" in twenty-two cities (and these include cities like Savannah, San Francisco, New Orleans, Saint Paul, Charleston, etc., where very few young children are employed) we find that 4,938 children, between six and eleven years of age, are employed, and another 3,503, between thirteen and fourteen; 2,793, between fourteen and fifteen, and 2,271, between fifteen and sixteen. In all, in only 22 cities, 13,505 children, between *six* and sixteen, working in factories or workshops, and this takes no account of Domestic Industries (Ibid., pp. 178–79).

"As a matter of fact ... the Reports of the State Superintendent of Instruction show not only that the percentage of children enrolled, and attending the public schools, has been comparatively small, but that, with the exception of the year 1886, there has been a gradual but very perceptible falling off since 1879. ... Every age-period has been affected, which is evidence that want of school accommodation ... does not account for this apparent deterioration" (New Jersey, 1888, p. 623). "Our whole provision for the care of the children of the working class is far inferior to that of England" (F. Kelley Wichnewetzsky, in *The Press*, June 1889).

Now as to the condition of the women. Generally, "the figures tell a sad story," says the Commissioner on the "Condition of Women in Large Cities" (p. 70 of his Report). And he adds, "One is forced to ask how women can live on such earnings." "Wages are low and almost beggarly" (Indianapolis, ibid., p. 18). "As a rule the establishments in which the girls work are not well calculated for industrial uses. Many of them are without proper means of escape in case of fire, many have no dressing-rooms or closets, and most are neither sufficiently lighted nor properly ventilated" (Ibid.). In Georgia, "the cost of living is comparatively high ... wages, except in the dry goods stores, are generally low." In Brooklyn, "though not so crowded as New York, the life conditions are almost as hard. Whole streets and districts are given over to poverty, filth, and vice, the sanitary and moral unwholesomeness of which is manifest. Better homes distinguish the districts remote from the business centers, but the great distance of these homes is a tax as to hours and [street] car fares" (p. 15). Of the life of the New York Seamstress we have spoken in an earlier chapter. "Out West" they would not seem to be much better off. "The poorest class of women in San Francisco are the seamstresses. A number of institutions were discovered by the agent of the Department, where a regular system of fraud was being practiced upon the defenseless sewing women." And like their sisters in the north and east, the San Francisco sewing women have now formed a union for their protection and "to prevent such frauds and prosecute when perpetrated" (p. 26).

Under the head of "Earnings and Lost Time" we find that taking the weekly average for 22 cities, representing practically the whole of the States, women earn $5.24, or about 21 shillings, but of these women (altogether 5,716) 373 earn less than 20 a year, 1,212 from 20 to 30, that is between 8 and 12 shillings a week. Nor must it be forgotten that the comparatively high and "fair" wage of 21 shillings represents considerably less in America, where living and rent are dearer, than it would be with us. Of the total number of women who gave income and expenditure, 682 received an income from other sources than their regular occupations. The expenses of these women were for rooms and meals 32 8s. 3d.; their total expenses 57 8s. 3d. As to the general condition of female labor it is quite clear, from the various investigations that have been made, that there is little, if any improvement in the amount of earnings which a woman can secure by working in the industries open to her; her earnings seem not only ridiculously low, but dangerously so" (p. 72).

How "dangerous" is shown by the reports on prostitution. The "partial" investigation on this subject is far from complete. But the "number of prostitutes as stated . . . falls far below the total number of prostitutes" in the cities under investigation. "Thus in Chicago, for example, there are, or were at the time of the investigation . . . 302 houses of ill-fame, assignation-houses, and 'rooming' houses . . . known to the police, containing 1,097 inmates," while the investigation involved "only 557 of this number." An interesting fact for those who consider housework as the one proper field for women's labor is that of the 3,866 prostitutes who "gave information," almost the largest number come under the head of having been employed in "house work, hotel work, table work, and cooking." Of these there were 1,155. The most numerous class ("a fact which strikes one sadly" says the Commissioner—for does it not show what working-class homes are?—"is the large number who enter prostitution directly from their homes") are those given as having "no previous occupation"—1,236. Dressmaker, seamstresses, employees in cloak and shirt factories, button-hole makers, are next on the sad list with 505; then come saleswomen and cashiers with 126. We need not go through the whole list. But for the benefit of those virtuous persons who would close theaters and all places of amusement, we may add that under the rather general heading of "actresses, ballet-girls, circus performers, singers, etc." the number given is only 52. Thus those very occupations supposed to be specially adapted to women contribute 29.88 percent of the whole number of prostitutes comprehended in this summary.

It should also be noted that in spite of the "dangerously low wages," in spite of the hideously immoral surroundings of these working women's lives "they do not recruit the houses of prostitution—and the virtuous character of our working women is all the more attractive when the cost of their virtue is recognized" (p. 77).

As to the wages, hours, and conditions of work generally. In Massachusetts, "in all industries considered together the average yearly earnings were 80 10s. 0d., the highest average appearing in cooking, lighting and heating apparatus, namely, 158 yearly. The only other industry averaging yearly earnings above 140 is chemical preparations, 141 8s. 0d. . . . in six industries the average earnings were between 120 and 140; in seven, between 100 and 120; in thirteen industries the average ranged from 80 to 100; and in eleven industries the range was from 60 to 80. In two industries the average fell below 60. In Massachusetts this average of 80 10s. 0d. is higher than the average in 1887, which was 78 19s. 2d., but this is largely due to the higher wage in certain special branches of industry and more constant work (Statistics of Manufactures, 1888, Mass., pp. 115–18).

The hours of labor are still terribly long in America. In 31 different trades reported upon in the New Jersey Report for 1888, in

17 industries the employees worked 59 hours; in five, 60; in one, 59.5; in two, 58; in four, between 57.25 and 57.75; in one, 56; and in one, 54, this being the least number of hours. In certain other States, the working day would be found even longer. Railway employees everywhere work shamefully long hours. Thus Minnesota has found it necessary to enact that, "on all lines of railroad, the time of labor of locomotive engineers and fireman shall not, at any time, exceed 18 hours a day, unless in case of accident or unavoidable delay." Working 18 hours, what wonder railway accidents are frequent! And in these accidents 55 percent of the victims are employees, "to whom the railroad is a veritable Juggernaut." "One in every 344 employees engaged in working railroads, and not including general officers, clerks, and shopmen, met with an accidental death—a record which is startling enough without taking into consideration the large number, who, while not fatally injured, were maimed to a greater or less extent. . . . In the United Kingdom . . . the casualty rate has not been so high as with us since 1875" (New Jersey, 1888, pp. 7, 8).

And, with these long hours, the intensity of work, as we have pointed out earlier, is far greater than in England. Mr. Shearman, in the *Star*, says, on 9 June 1890: "Every workman is expected to produce a great deal more in proportion than in England. He must work more rapidly; he is required to apply himself with an intensity which is unknown here, and as the result, where wages are 25 percent higher, he produces from 50 to 75 percent more goods, and where the wages are 100 percent higher, he produced 150 percent more than the corresponding English workman. This is true of the general average. Of course, there are some cases in which it is not true, but they are quite a small minority. A man who only does poor and slow work, will get as small wages in America as he probably would in England. For example, in Lancashire, so far as I know, a weaver who attends to four looms in a cotton mill is supposed to do very good work, but the same class of weaver, emigrating from Lancashire to Massachusetts, would be required to run eight looms at one time. Doing thus double the amount of work, he would, nevertheless, receive an advance of wages, at the most, not exceeding 40 percent—probably less. I do not know what the returns now are in Manchester. But, some years ago, there was a trade union formed for the purpose of regulating the amount of work the men should do, and they would not allow their members to lay more than 1,000 bricks a day. The very same men who had been engaged there in that work emigrated to New York, and, in flush times, received double the wages they had received in England, but not one of them could obtain work unless on condition of laying, at least, 3,000 bricks a day, which was the minimum.

With hours, at least, as long—and very often longer—with the cost of living, especially in the matter of rent, far higher than in England, no wonder Mr. Shearman adds, "Wages in America are really lower than in England."

And while, on the one side, the working hours are so long, the number of unemployed is on the increase. "In 1887, the average number employed in all the establishments represented (in the State of Massachusetts) was 172,208, and the average number employed in the same establishments, in 1888, was 172,796. This indicates a slight increase in the average number employed; but the number of persons employed at periods of employment of the greatest number shows an increase of only 0.55 percent in 1888, while the number of employed for periods of employment of the smallest numbers shows a decrease of 1.42 percent. The range of nonemployment was, therefore, greater in 1888 than in 1887" (Statistics of Manufactures, Mass., 1888, p. 146).

The inflicting of fines continues to be a matter of constant complaint. "Another subject, which has engaged the attention of the bureau, is the practice in certain factories, shops, and stores of imposing fines upon certain employees for trivial offenses, created by arbitrary rules. . . . The levying of a fine constitutes an infringement upon the stipulated wages, and is equivalent to a seizure by force of money already earned. . . . In effect, these fines, though each be a small amount in itself, when aggregated in a large establishment, constitute a considerable sum to the credit of the firm, for which no equivalent is rendered" (Michigan, 1890, p. 326). "The system of fining (in Cincinnati) works great hardships among the shopgirls. . . . Fines are common (in Providence), sometimes becoming a heavy grievance" (Women in Large Cities, pp. 17, 23).

But of all complaints the most bitter are against the horrible danger from fire to which American workers are exposed. Not only is it quite common to lock in hundreds of hands, "but unless absolutely forced by the inspectors, the employers neglect the most elementary precautions." Speaking in the August of 1889 at the Convention of Factory Inspectors, Mr. White of Massachusetts said: "It would be very little use to put a fire-escape on a powder-house, and hundreds of the buildings now occupied for tenement and lodging-houses would, under favorable circumstances, burn down so quickly as to render nearly useless any means of escape that can be provided. The late fire in a tenement house (factory) in New York is a striking example of the terrible results of such methods of construction."

Inspector Dorn says in his Ohio report: "Most of the buildings are improperly constructed with reference to egress, the ingenuity of the architect having apparently been exerted to secure the greatest possible economy of space in the matter of stairways. . . . Many of the buildings used for shops and factories are from four to seven stories high, and generally the first three or four floors of the buildings are used as storerooms, the employees using the upper floors, escape from which would, in most cases, be extremely difficult in the event of a rapidly spreading fire, and loss of life and serious bodily injury almost inevitable. Some of these buildings are supplied with but a single stairway, and where there are two or more they are generally located so near together that a fire which would render any of them useless as an avenue of escape would be very likely to do so with all. In many cases, also, these stairways are located near elevators, which are most potent aids to the rapid progress of fire."

And in his 1887 report: "In a good many instances parties have provided buildings with straight ladders, which are frequently useless, especially where there are women employed, and in many instances even men cannot use them. Other parties, again, have provided wooden ladders, claiming that the law does not specify the material to be used."

Inspector Schaubert of New York reports: "I find some fire escapes made of gas-pipe bent and driven into the wall that would require a trapeze performer to ascend them. For instance, in Rochester, two buildings, seven stories high. In one there are usually 150 and in the other about 270 female operatives employed on the top floors. But one stairway in each connects the various stories. In the rear of these structures, I find these gas pipe arrangements for fire escape. . . . Another alleged fire-escape is that in the rear of a certain printing-house. About sixty females are here employed in the fifth floor. Only one narrow staircase runs from the top of the building to the street, and in the rear a straight ladder extends from the top to the second floor. This ladder would be almost valueless in case a panic should seize the work-women."

Most persons on reading these facts will be inclined to say

with Mr. Dorn, "It is somewhat difficult to speak with calmness of men who, while liberally insuring their property against fire, so that in case of such a visitation—a danger always imminent—their pockets shall not suffer, will not spend a dollar for the security of the lives of those by whose labor they profit."

A few words in concluding these notes on strikes and lockouts. The admirable volume prepared by the Washington Commissioner, Mr. Carroll D. Wright, deserves a more exhaustive analysis than we have space for. We can quote but a few figures, but they are eloquent as to the relations of labor and capital in the bourgeois Eldorado.

RELATIVE NUMBER OF STRIKES BY YEARS

Year	Strikes	Establishments	Employees striking and involved
1881	471	2928	129,521
1882	454	2105	154,671
1883	478	2759	149,763
1884	443	2367	147,054
1885	645	2284	242,705
1886	1,411	9861	499,489
	3902	22,304	1,323,203

From further statistics to hand it seems that strikes in the beginning of 1887 at all events were on the decline.

"So far as gaining the objects for which the strikes or lockouts were instituted is concerned, it is shown by the summaries that for the strikes out of the whole number of establishments affected, viz., 22,304, success followed in 10,375 establishments, or 46.52 percent of the whole; partial success was gained in 3,004, or 13.47 percent of the whole, and failure followed in 8910 establishments or 39.95 percent of the whole number" (Strikes and Lock-outs, p. 16).

But while the successful strikes related to 46.52 percent of the whole establishments, the number of strikers involved in these successful strikes was only 39.19 percent of the whole number; partially successful strikes account for 13.47 percent of the involved establishments and only 10.88 percent of the persons; and the failures that occurred in 39.95 percent of all the establishments involved 49.91 percent of the strikers (p. 17). Although it is impossible to ascertain quite accurately the relative loss of employers and employees, Mr. Wright finds on taking the information supplied, that "the loss to the strikers during the period involved was 10,362,945. The loss to employees through lockouts was 1,631,543; or a total wage loss to employees of 11,994,488. This loss occurred for both strikes and lockouts in 24,518 establishments, or an average loss of 489 to each establishment, and of over £8 to each person involved" (p. 18).

Not the least interesting of the "Tables" drawn up in this report are those showing "the amount of time necessary for the strikers to regain, through increased wages, what they had lost in wages during the strike." The strikes included are those for increase of wage which were successful or partly successful. "The time required for the successful strikers to meet the wage loss occurring during the strike is 76 days; that is, the successful strikers would have to work 76 days at the increase gained by the strike to recover the losses incurred during the strike.... the partly successful strikers... would require 361 days... the two classes together would require 99 working days." Facts certainly that strengthen the argument of those who assure certain improvements in the lot of the workers by legal enactment rather than by the slow, costly, and very doubtful means of strikes.

Finally, some extracts that sum up the whole position of the wage-worker, not only in America, but in every "civilized" country, from the remarks of Mr. Edward J. Kean, chief clerk of the New York Labor Bureau. Dealing with the question of wages and general condition of the workers, Mr. Kean says: "The efficiency of the worker has also to be taken into account. Formerly, an employer might pick out a man of unusual merit, and give him an unusual rate; but such a practice is no longer favored. The unions think a regular wage for all is a better guarantee for the body of workers than the capricious or interested liberality of the employer. They prefer uniformity. . . . There is certainly a broad line of demarcation between educated expert and plain laborers; but between proficients the lines of wage-worths are arbitrary. That the work of the worker is not always a material element in estimating the wage rate is shown in the difference of amount between woman's and man's wages . . . even where equal excellence is presumable. . . . The sum is usually quoted to show the wage earnings; the real point is, however, the purchasing power of the wages. . . . Almost all accidents are at the worker's own risk . . . these are regarded as incidents of the calling, and so they are, but what if caused by the neglect of proper and reasonable care? . . . Again, risky or offensive callings, by a perversion of social equity, poorly paid; as if performed by the pariahs of society. In railroad accidents the passenger is indemnified, but the employee is put in the position of a joint contractor, and gets no relief for hurt or damage. . . . In factories and other labor aggregations, the theoretic wage idea seems to be, 'How little will keep the working animal in working condition.' "

Note to Chapters 8 and 10

A few additional words on the various Organizations in America, on the position of certain well-known men, notably Mr. Powderly and Mr. Henry George, and on the Chicago Anarchists.

The fairly obvious prophecies made, when we were writing in 1887, have, within the short space of less than three years, been in the main realized. The split in the Knights of Labor that was foretold has occurred. The conservative, reactionary, Powderly portion of that organization has gone over very much more completely to the reactionary side, just as their English prototypes, Messrs. Broadhurst and Shipton, have given themselves and the cause of their fellow-workers away, for the sake of being in with the respectable middleclass.

The Central Labor Union also has, to a large extent, disappeared, or rather been absorbed into the new and important organization—the [American] Federation of Labor. This organization is also absorbing the best elements of the Knights of Labor. Two of the most prominent men in this Federation are P. J. McGuire, already mentioned by us as an energetic and thorough worker, and Mr. [Samuel] Gompers.

The Germans to whom we referred as not understanding the movement in the States, holding aloof from the Knights of Labor and the Central Labor Unions, and anxious to "boss the show" in America, have curiously and very completely justified our words. The men to whom we referred are now discredited in their own party in America, and the guidance of affairs has been taken out of their hands; and although the German part in the American movement, and with that the spread of Socialism, has been seriously hindered and hampered by their action and inaction, there seems every prospect that now the German Socialists in America understand how essential it is that the movement there must be American as well as international, and will work in that understanding with their American brethren.

Henry George and his party count now for nothing serious in the labor movement in America; the single-tax idea is played out.

And we cannot but think that precisely the same historic fate awaits the Nationalists with their high priest, Mr. [Edward] Bellamy.* Mr. Bellamy has drunk deeply at the well of [the German socialist leader and author of *Woman and Socialism*, August]

---

*Edward Bellamy's work of utopian fiction, *Looking Backward, 2000–1887* (Boston: Houghton Mifflin and Co., 1889) had a powerful impact in the United States, exciting great interest in socialism as a more efficient and ethical form of society which was supposedly being brought about by the dynamics of the great capitalist corporations themselves—views taken up by the so-called "Nationalist" movement inspired by his novel. We can see in the Marx-Aveling comments that at least some Marxist-influenced socialists were not positively impressed. William Morris's great utopian novel *News From Nowhere*—contained in *News From Nowhere and Other Writings*, ed. Clive Wilmer (London: Penguin Books, 1993)—picturing socialism as a profoundly democratic-libertarian society to be won through a working-class revolution—was written, in part, as a response to and rejection of Bellamy's orientation, which is subjected to an uncompromising left-wing assault in Arthur Lipow's scholarly *Authoritarian Socialism in America: Edward Bellamy and the Nationalist Movement* (Berkeley: University of

Bebel, so deeply that he has forgotten the source of his inspiration. The only portions of his book that of any value are taken directly from Bebel, but they are marred in the taking. Mr. Bellamy's Boston woman in Mr. Bellamy's ideas state is anything but Bebel's Frau in der Zukunft [woman of the future].

It would be idle to deny that Mr. Bellamy's book [*Looking Backward*] has made a sensation amongst the middle class—a sensation curiously parallel to that produced by a very similar book, Mr. Drummond's *Natural Law in the Spiritual World*. Both works serve to reassure the bourgeois mind. In the case of Mr. Drummond's, it was necessary to show that Evolution was, after all, very harmless, and by no means incompatible with bourgeois Christian belief. In similar fashion, Mr. Bellamy dreams a dream, in which he sees that the coming changes in society are harmless enough, and are not likely to disturb the dominant position of the middle class. Mr. Bellamy reassures himself and his cothinkers with the belief that the great social and economic change impending will be brought about not by the working class, but by such middle-class folk as the Nationalists and the Fabian Society.

California Press, 1982). Far more positive assessments of Bellamy can be found in: Franklin Rosemont, "Free Play and No Limit: An Introduction to Edward Bellamy's Utopia," in Paul Buhle, ed., *Popular Culture in America* (Minneapolis: University of Minnesota Press, 1987); Franklin Rosemont, "Bellamy's Radicalism Reclaimed," in Daphne Paul, ed. *Looking Backward, 1988–1888* (Amherst: University of Massachusetts Press, 1988); Csaba Toth, "Utopianism as Americanism," *American Quarterly* 45, no. 4 (December 1993): 649–58; and Csaba Toth, "Transatlantic Dialogue: Nineteenth Century American Utopianism and Europe," Ph.D. Dissertation, University of Minnesota, 1992. German socialist leader August Bebel had written a profound and famous book in 1878—a later U.S. translation by Daniel DeLeon took the inaccurate title *Woman Under Socialism* (New York: Schocken Books, 1971)—which went through many editions and portrayed socialism in a manner that influenced many like Bellamy who nonetheless rejected the book's Marxist orientation.

THE CHICAGO ANARCHISTS

In spite of the efforts made in America, in England, on the Continent of Europe, to bring the American authorities to something like a reasonable consideration of the crime and the blunder they were committing, four of the Chicago Anarchists were judicially murdered in Cook county jail in November 1887. It was a cowardly and brutal murder, in keeping with the habits of a nation that executes a man (by a novel method—electricity for choice) after keeping him in prison two or three years.

The petitions on behalf of the Chicago Anarchists, condemned not because their guilt was proven, but because they were Anarchists, were signed in England by hundreds of men and women who had no sympathy with, but rooted antipathy to, Anarchism. In America and in Chicago itself, they were signed by thousands on thousands. And now let us tell so much of the English public as we may have for readers the story told us, when we revisited the States in 1888, by those who knew the ins and outs of that most murderous business. Even in America, even in Chicago, a revulsion of feeling had set in favor of the men condemned on no real evidence. In the city itself, petitions were being signed like wild fire in the offices of the business men, in the restaurants, the clubs, everywhere. From all parts of America and the world they were flowing in. The Governor of the State of Illinois, in whose hands (oh, mockery!) were the lives of seven human beings—Neebe had been sentenced to 15 years' jail, the death sentences on Schwab and Fielden commuted to hard labor for life—was known to be wavering.

It was time for the police to act. And this is what they did. The warder that had been attending the cell where Lingg—the youngest and the wildest of the Anarchists—was lodged, through the long months of imprisonment, was suddenly removed. A new man was put in his place, and within the hour almost, the bombs were most opportunely in Lingg's cell. It was significant that the police, admittedly greedy for the lives of these men, found these bombs just as bombs were discovered in the streets of Chicago whenever public interest in the trial waned.

The next morning Chicago, America, were aflame. The vile Anarchists were at their old games again. The signing of petitions ceased. Names were withdrawn. The governor confirmed the sentence of death on four of the men yet left—one American and three Germans.

It was absolutely impossible with the police precautions that were taken for any one of the prisoners to get bombs into his cell without the knowledge of the police. And, in the case of Lingg, anything of the sort was even less likely than with any of the rest. It was perfectly well known that Lingg wanted to die on the scaffold, had prepared the speech he intended to make, and was looking forward to the hour of his martyrdom.

And the warder that had been with Lingg all the earlier months disappeared. Captain Black, the advocate for the men, moved heaven and earth to find him—but nothing came of it.

We have no hesitation in saying that but for that discovery of these bombs in Lingg's cell, his companions would not have been hanged, and nothing will induce the friends of the men to believe either than that the bombs were introduced into his cell by the police.

Essay
After the "Tour"
Kim Moody

Edward and Eleanor Marx Aveling could hardly have picked a more significant moment to visit the United States and tour its budding working-class movement. Eighteen eighty-six was both a high point and a turning point for the fledgling U.S. labor movement. Certainly, it was a high point of independent working-class political action. The eight-hour strike of 1886—America's first and as yet only national general strike—brought hundreds of thousands of workers to the streets on May 1. Independent labor candidates ran in scores of industrial cities and won in some. At the same time, both the Knights of Labor and the new craft unions were on the upswing. But the optimistic picture of growing working-class radicalism and organization the Avelings painted could not foretell the more rocky path American workers would have to tread.

The Working-Class Movement in America is unique in its Marxist outlook and focus on the working class. Yet even the famous daughter of Karl Marx and her husband were people of their time. They came to the United States naive about a system of race relations still in the making and peculiar to the western hemisphere. Also, they had been schooled in an optimistic version of Marxism consistent with the positive view of the world current in the Victorian Britain from which they came. Their work is significant for what they saw: the incredible poverty, the intensification of labor that foretold of a changing system of work, and the rise of a confused, yet exciting and growing working-class movement. But it is also significant for what they missed. Only a hint of troubled times comes through in the notes from their 1887 return to America on the desperate case of the Haymarket anarchists, whose defense the Avelings militantly embraced, and the split in the Knights of Labor. The fact is, their statement in the appendix to the 1891 edition, that "the relative positions of Labor and Capital are in this year, 1890, the same as they were when we wrote—only more so," was wrong.

By the early 1890s, the Knights were reduced to near extinction. According to their own records, membership in the Knights fell from its 1886 high point of 729,677 to a mere 74,635 in 1893. The new AFL craft unions grew, but only slowly from 140,000 in 1886 to 275,000 in 1893. Furthermore, the political character of organized labor became decidedly less radical. The socialism of early craft unionists like Peter J. McGuire was being transformed into "pure and simple unionism," the forerunner of American business unionism. Indeed, in the early 1890s, the "unconscious socialism" the Avelings had described was inundated by the populism they also saw forming in the Grange of the 1880s. By 1896, however, even populism's momentary class independence collapsed as that movement endorsed silver currency advocate William Jennings Bryan on the Democratic Party ticket.

To be sure, the employers' offensive unleashed after the Haymarket incident met with the kind of heroic resistance the Avelings would have admired. Strikes at Homestead and Pullman in 1892 and 1894 respectively are synonymous with monumental class struggle. And, of course, the Pullman strike produced America's most famous socialist leader, Eugene V. Debs. In fact, 1894 saw more strike activity than 1886. But as the Avelings pointed out, whereas some 60 percent of the strikes in 1886 were whole or partial successes, virtually all of the strikes of 1894 ended in defeat. By 1896, America's working-class movement was smaller and largely limited to skilled workers. It was also distinctly narrower in the political and social outlook of most of its leadership. There would be a return of working-class radicalism and militancy as well as impressive union growth after 1900, but the rise of American labor was not to be simple or linear.

What happened after the "tour" is not only of historical interest. The forces and trends that threw labor off the course the Avelings foresaw speak directly to our times and the plight of the U.S. working class today. Three enormous changes occurred during the last two decades of the nineteenth century and the first decade of the twentieth century for which the fledgling movement of 1886 was not prepared. First was one of the many sea changes in race relations in the United States that tended to carve racism deeper into national life, making it not only a feature of backward rural Southern life, but of the development of the United States as a modern industrial nation. Second was the development of an integrated national economy dominated by giant corporations and the transformation of the workplace they engineered in the name of "scientific management." Third were the waves of immigration that constantly renewed and altered the working class itself, particularly after 1900. Together, these tidal forces redrew the social and industrial map of America.

The Avelings noted the "split" of the craft unions from the

Knights in their "Note to Chapter 8 and 10," but saw it as a progressive departure from the "Conservative, reactionary Powderly portion" of the Knights. Despite the residual marxism of some of their leaders, however, the craft unions that formed the American Federation of Labor also represented a departure from the rudimentary racial and gender egalitarianism of the Knights and its inclusion of all workers regardless of national origin or skills. The Knights lacked the structure, class vision, and organizational roots in the workplace needed to survive a period of drastic employer repression and industrial restructuring. But their egalitarian inclusiveness pointed to a key element required to organize the nationwide, capital-intensive industries that came to dominate America's economic landscape.

The craft unions, on the other hand, were predominantly organizations of skilled white men of western European heritage. Although, as David Montgomery has pointed out, they were capable of mounting impressive solidarity between themselves and in moments of crisis even with unskilled workers, they came increasingly to accept the narrowness of their organizations as the very secret of their success. Although their leaders frequently spoke the language of class, in practice they internalized an exclusive ethnic, racial, and elite occupational vision of that class that "experience" appeared to justify. Events beyond the reach of the leaders and members of the emerging craft unions helped shape this distorted idea of class and narrow conception of labor organization.

The Compromise of 1877, which ended Reconstruction, withdrew federal troops from the South and unleashed the forces of white supremacy around the nation. African Americans were to be held in Southern peonage by disenfranchisement, legal segregation, and violence in the South and by the agreement of northern Republican industrialists not to employ Black labor. This meant that the emerging industrial economy in the North was to be largely populated by white workers drawn from American workers and farmers or European immigrants until the accelerated "global" demand created by the coming of the First World War. For all the exceptions, this pattern meant that racial exclusion from or segregation within the new industries and the corporate organizations that dominated them would appear to many craft unionists as the "natural" order of economic life as a truly national economy took shape around them.

Just as women had long been excluded from skilled wage labor by a presumed natural order of the genders in the family, so the segregation of Blacks and Asians in unskilled jobs or to work in local transport or services could be viewed as "the way things are." A politically determined contemporary reality thus reenforced a more ancient prejudice rooted in the division of Black and white labor in the era of slavery. Organized labor became, in the minds of its leaders and majority, even more than in its real composition, white labor. It stood in precarious isolation from existing Black labor and its later migrations that would change strategic sectors of the industrial workforce from the First World War on.

The ideology of skill as the basis of organizational stability also had certain roots in the reality of late nineteenth-century America. Through panic and recovery the organizations of craftsmen in the building trades could maintain a hold on the local markets in which many were still employed. Indeed, the "skyscraper" downtowns created by the rising national corporations as early as the 1880s gave union construction workers a greater sense of power in the new industrial and financial centers like Chicago, Pittsburgh, and St. Louis. Even inside the new industries, skilled machinists, iron and steel makers, electricians, and others associated with the "new technology" in production and transportation were better able to resist the antiunion offensive of the employers than the unskilled workers who were becoming the majority of the industrial workforce. The very exclusiveness of unions like the Machinists and Amalgamated Iron and Steel Workers seemed to give them the bargaining power and organizational stability the polyglot Knights had lacked. Even after the defeat at Homestead, the craft unions made headway. The "boom" from 1898 through 1903 saw the craft unions in many of the new giants like General Electric, International Harvester, and U.S. Steel make gains in both organization and wages.

Nevertheless, the reorganization of production under the financial umbrella of the giant corporations at the national level and the accelerated introduction of Frederick Winslow Taylor's "scientific management" in the workplace at the opening of the twentieth century issued a challenge to craft unionism for which it had no enduring answer. The local and metropolitan area bargaining patterns of the craft unions could not hold up in a national market dominated by centralized finance and industrial capital. The isolation of skilled workers from the majority of unskilled operatives undermined the bargaining power inherent in skill. Major recessions in 1897 and 1903 handed the employers the tool to attack many of the craft unions. Taylorism came to replace the union rule book. The sheer weight of immigrant operatives and laborers in many of the industries that fed America's emerging consumer society and the miserable conditions that persisted into the twentieth century meant that craft unionism could not hold the line for itself much less the rest of the class even as it understood that class.

The recovery of 1904 and later the rise of demand from European powers preparing for war provided U.S. labor as a whole its opportunity. The immigrant laborers and operatives, a growing number of them women, began to form their own organizations. Such diverse unions as the International Ladies Garment Workers Union, the Amalgamated Clothing Workers, the United Shoe Workers, and the Industrial Workers of World swelled with the ranks of immigrant workers. Ironically, the rebellion of the diverse and unskilled probably saved the craft unions, some of which began to open their doors to their less-skilled brothers and, occasionally, sisters.

The remarkable labor upheaval and radicalization from 1904 through 1919 would certainly have been seen by the Avelings as justification for their optimism had they lived to see it. Unions, old and new, grew by leaps and bounds. Unskilled Black and white longshore workers closed the port of New Orleans in 1907, explicitly under the banner of Black-white unity. Craft unionists demanded and, in some cases, created amalgamated organizations of all trades within a company or large scale workplace. Shop committees and other forms of workplace union power confronted the effects of "scientific management." The Socialist Party and the IWW appeared to be growing apace.

The labor movement that emerged toward the end of the First World War, however, not only contained the seeds of a new working-class movement, but the virus of the old. Craft unions continued to dominate the labor movement and the ideology of exclusion tenaciously merged with the new ideology of business unionism. Samuel Gompers and other AFL leaders posed as industrial statesmen in alliance with capital as members of the National Civic Federation. Many of these top leaders made little effort to conceal their contempt of Asians, Blacks, or the new immigrants from southern and eastern Europe. When the climactic confrontations with the Robber Baron bastions came in meatpacking in 1918–1919 and steel in 1919, craft rivalry, ethnic antagonism, and racial hostility paved the road to defeat. Coalitions of craft unions carefully constructed by radical syndicalist William Z. Foster in both these industries crumbled in the face of resistance from the commanding heights of capital, whose strategists were not shy in playing the racial card. Race riots exploded in East Chicago in 1917 and in Chicago and fourteen other cities in the summer of 1919, destroying unionism in the stockyards and undermining the nationwide steel strike of that September. In the wake of this defeat government repression destroyed the IWW, marginalized the craft unions in heavy industry, and mortally weakened the already splintered socialist movement. The AFL failed to do what genuine industrial unionism would do two decades later throughout basic industry. This failure, in turn, abetted the decline and isolation of the socialist left for a decade. Not until the 1930s Depression would a radical resurgence accompany the rise of the Congress of Industrial Organizations.

ANOTHER TRANSFORMATION, ANOTHER BUSINESS— UNIONISM, ANOTHER RACIAL DIVIDE

Once again, labor is in crisis in the United States. The industrial union organizations inherited from the CIO upheaval of the 1930s and 1940s have been dwindling for three decades and the proportion of workers in unions has reached the level of the late 1920s. As of 1992, only 11.5 percent of the workers in the private sector belonged to unions. Public sector workers held on at about 35 percent. The weakening power of the unions was expressed in declining wage increases from about 10 percent in the early 1980s to less than 3 percent in the late 1980s and early 1990s. Real wages in America remained below the levels of the early 1970s. In spite of the many concessions on work rules and benefits made by unions in the private sector, the major corporations continued to "downsize" and "re-engineer" away tens of thousands of union jobs.

Today's context is, of course, different from that of the late nineteenth century. For one thing, the United States led a global trend toward declining profit rates, seeing its own rates of return on capital stock fall to a third of those of the 1960s. For another, America is not a rising industrial upstart, but a declining mature economic power. U.S. manufacturing fell from 35 percent of the total production of the world's market economies in 1970 to 25 percent in the late 1980s, while rising Japan gained some 9 percentage points. The U.S. share of world merchandise trade slipped from 16 percent in 1966 to 14 percent in 1986. But probably the most confounding change from labor's point of view has been the trend toward "globalization" of economic activity that accompanied the crisis of profitability and the fall from economic dominance.

If the youthful labor movement witnessed by the Avelings faced the growth of national corporations and markets, today's aging U.S. trade unions confront transnational corporations; the rise of huge regionalized international markets in Europe, North America, and East Asia; and the unfolding of internationalized systems of production. The wages and benefits of U.S. workers must not only be competitive with those in Europe or Japan, but increasingly with workers in the Third World, as global producers move more work to sites of production in maquiladora plants in Mexico or Guatemala or to "free trade zones" in Asia or the Caribbean. In these enclaves of production workers earn $4 a day or less. Although there are some limits on what types of production can be moved to such sites, the threat of plant closings remains a powerful tool in extracting concessions from U.S. workers. Intensified competition among the transnational corporations in the troubled major markets provides the incentive for increased pressure on labor everywhere.

Similarly, the conditions of the contemporary workplace are increasingly set at the global level. Transnational corporations, according to the United Nations, now account for about one-quarter of the manufacturing value produced in the world. In this "TNC universe," as the UN calls it, it is the "lean" production system developed in Japan that sets the standard worldwide. Following the example pioneered by Taiichi Ohno of Toyota Motors, new technology, flexible work rules, just-in-time parts delivery, and increased international outsourcing and subcontracting of phases of production are replacing the system of centralized mass production so familiar to unions in North America and Europe. Flexible systems of work are today's version of the "scientific management." Enthusiasts of schemes like Team Concept, Total Quality Management, and Synchronous Manufacturing, as some of the workplace manifestations of "lean" production are called, see these as the opposite of Taylorism. Yet, the end result is much the same: speed-up, deskilling, and the rise of new industrial diseases such as repetitive motion injuries. It is today's version of what the Avelings called "the greater intensity of labor in America."

Altogether, the new systems of production emerging in the United States as a result of globalization bear a frightening resemblance to some of the trends in the late nineteenth century. For one thing, "sweated labor" and sweatshops have returned as the downside of "lean" production. In 1888, a British Royal Commission noted that sweated labor appeared "very largely wherever the system of subcontracting prevails." This describes today's garment and electronics sweatshops in New York, San Francisco, Los Angeles, Silicon

Valley, El Paso, and others where immigrant women workers labor in substandard conditions and are sometimes even cheated of any pay by contract employers. It also describes the army of one and a half-million temporaries employed by labor agencies in the United States, or the millions of part-timers in service jobs who make minimum wage with few or no benefits.

Another frightening aspect of these changes is the racial and gender stratification that goes with them. The new sweatshop and contract workers in manufacturing and service jobs are disproportionately people of color, many of them immigrant women. Global economic reorganization has created the largest recorded labor migration in history. According to the International Labor Organization (ILO) some 100 million people are in migration on any given day. Naturally, many are moving inexorably toward the centers of better pay and available jobs. Globalization appears not only as something external to the nation, but once again as a transformation of the working class at home.

As capital intensive industrial production has moved from urban centers to suburban or exurban peripheries, better-paying jobs have become fewer and more white in ethnicity. Immigrants and dislocated native-born workers of color compete for low income work in and around decaying urban centers. Growing service industries like health care contain an internal occupational stratification that reflects the nation's retreat from the goal of racial and gender equality. There is the danger that once again, racial and gender segregation in employment will appear as the "natural" way of the new economic order, providing the justification for a self-defeating defensive narrowness.

All too often, American unions have responded to the new context by reverting to this sort of narrowness, on the one hand, and a new "statesmanship," on the other. Job security programs that protect only high seniority workers and trade protectionism meant to shield union employers are one side of this response. Contract concessions and the embrace of labor-management cooperation schemes in the name of competitiveness are another. Both approaches promise only isolation from the vast majority of the unorganized U.S. working class and those workers abroad who are part of the internationalized systems of production. The labor movement must find a way to breach the racial and gender divisions within the U.S. working class, to incorporate the contemporary massive wave of immigration, and to reach beyond its national setting to function in today's internationalized markets and systems of production.

For labor in the United States this means returning to the idea that is the title of the Avelings' book: namely, a working-class movement in America. As labor educator Elaine Bernard frequently points out, only in the United States today does the term "labor movement" refer exclusively to trade unions. In Canada, Europe, Asia, and the Third World, as in the U.S. when the Avelings visited, labor movement usually means unions, associated working class-based political parties, an independent workers' press, and sometimes other kinds of mass organizations. The unions of today may provide a viable starting point for the construction of a genuine labor movement, but by themselves they cannot create something bold and broad enough to deal with the globalization from within and without. Reaching out to the millions of low-wage nonunion workers in the United States and to the organized and unorganized abroad will take the combined inclusive spirit of the Knight of Labor, the political daring and independence of the fledgling labor parties of the 1880s, and the international concern the Avelings brought to bear on American labor at a crucial moment in its history.

The Working-Class Movement in America provides us with a first-hand look at labor in the United States at a one of those rare and inspiring moments of class upheaval. It reminds us that socialism wasn't always a nasty word in labor circles and that people under even the most oppressive conditions can gain energy from the collective and democratic experience that is the labor movement at its best. If we are reminded of the need for a critical understanding of the vast global changes in capitalism and their impact on "the relative positions of Labor and Capital," it is also the case that "the working-class question" is, as the Avelings write in chapter 1, "always in essence the same, and for practical purposes may be put in these words: Why is it that the actual producers and distributors of wealth own the least wealth, and those who are not its actual producers and distributors own the most?"

SOURCES

Dubofsky, Melvyn, and Warren van Tine. *Labor Leaders in America*. Chicago: University of Illinois Press, 1987.

Fink, Leon. *Workingmen's Democracy: The Knights of Labor and American Politics*. Chicago: University of Illinois Press, 1983.

Montgomery, David. *The Fall of the House of Labor*. New York: Cambridge University Press, 1987.

———. *Workers' Control in America*. New York: Cambridge University Press, 1979.

United Nation Conference on Trade and Development. *World Investment Report 1993*. New York: United Nations, 1993.

Womack, James, Daniel Jones, and Daniel Roos. *The Machine That Changed the World*. New York: 1990.

World Bank 1990. *World Development Report*. Washington, D.C.: World Bank, 1990.

Index

Addams, Jane, 19
AFL-CIO, 20
African Americans, 11, 12, 13, 15, 85, 86, 108, 179, 211, 212
alcohol consumption and abuse, 113–14
Amalgamated Clothing Workers of America, 215
American Federation of Labor (AFL), 9, 18, 24, 47, 56, 203–204, 210, 211, 212, 215
American Railway Union, 15, 20
Anarchism and Socialism (Plekhanov), 42
anarchists and anarchism, 25, 54, 62, 63, 65, 80, 159–70, 180, 181, 182, 203, 206–207
Asian Americans, 13, 213
Aveling, Edward, 7, 8, 9, 11, 14, 16, 17, 22, 27, 39–41, 46, 47, 48, 49, 59, 60, 61, 64, 65, 209–12, 219
Avrich, Paul, 25

Bakunin, Mikhail, 168, 169
Balzac, Honore, 184
Banner, Robert, 60
"Battle Hymn of the Republic" (Julia Ward Howe), 182
Bebel, August, 204–205
Beecher, Henry Ward, 177
Bell, Daniel, 8, 24, 28
Bellamy, Edward, 204–205
Berlin, Ira, 23
Bernard, Elaine, 27, 220
Bernstein, Eduard, 60, 61
Besant, Walter, 78
Bensman, David, 26

223

Benson, Susan Porter, 26
Bismarck, Otto von, 58
Black, Captain William, 163, 166–67, 171, 180–82, 183, 187, 207
Blaine, James G., 156
Blake, Mrs. Devereux, 177
Bonfield, Captain John, 165
Boorstin, Daniel, 8, 28
boycotts, 93
Boyer, Richard O., 21, 35
Brier, Stephen, 26
Brotherhood of Carpenters, 19
Brotherhood of Sleeping Car Porters, 19
Brown, John, 179
Brundage, David, 26
Bryan, William Jennings, 210
Buhle, Mari Jo, 25
Buhle, Paul, 23, 24, 25, 205
Bureaus of Labor, 77, 81–83, 102, 107, 131, 136, 179, 186, 189, 190, 199, 201
Burns, Lizzie, 63

Campbell, Helen, 190
Capital (Marx), 60, 82, 83, 110
capitalism, 7–8, 9, 10–13, 14, 16–17, 18, 21, 32–33, 35, 52, 54, 69, 76–77, 78, 79, 80, 82–83, 131–32, 142, 147, 154, 172, 173, 190, 210–11, 212, 213, 214, 216–21
Central Labor Unions (Central Labor Councils), 80, 140, 145, 148, 167, 203, 204
Chamberlin, Brewster, 23
Chartists, 38, 178
Chidester, Davitt D., 175
Civil War, 12, 15, 137, 173, 179, 182
class consciousness and class struggle, 77, 78–80, 82, 116, 131–32, 133–36, 141–51, 154–58, 171–87, 209, 211. *See also* labor parties; labor press; socialism and socialists; strikes; trade unionism
Cold War, 8, 35
Coleman, Stephen, 147
Collier, Rev. Robert, 123
Commons, John R., 22
Communist Manifesto (Marx and Engels), 10, 53, 150, 169
Condition of the Working Class in England, The (Engels), 51, 53, 62, 82, 83, 190
Congress of Industrial Organizations (CIO), 20, 216
Constitution of the United States of America, 11, 12
Cooperative Commonwealth, The (Gronlund), 79
Cooperatives, 143
Countryman, Edward, 26
cowboys, 153–58
Cullen, Jim, 25

culture, 9, 25, 28, 48–50, 75–79

David, Henry, 25
Davis, Rebecca Harding, 78
Debs, Eugene V., 17, 20, 33–34, 211
DeLeon, Daniel, 147, 205
DeMille, Angela George, 171
Democratic Party, 10, 11, 15, 149, 150, 183, 210
Depression (1930s), 8, 216
Dickens, Charles, 78, 128
Disraeli, Benjamin, 78
Dixon, David, 27
Dolgoff, Sam, 169
Dollar Diplomacy, 17
Douglas, Dorothy, 190
Draper, Hal, 159
Drummond, Henry, 205
Dubinsky, David, 19, 33
Dubofsky, Melvyn, 10
Du Bois, W. E. B., 13, 29

education versus child labor, 124–27, 191–92
eight-hour movement, 9, 24, 44, 47, 83, 107, 132, 144, 209
Ely, Richard T., 134–35, 136, 138, 142
Engel, George, 169, 170
Engels, Frederick, 10–12, 13, 15, 16, 18, 20, 39, 41, 51, 53, 54, 56, 60, 61–62, 81, 82–83, 169

Eynon, Bret, 26

Faber, Seymour, 26
Fabian Society, 205
farmers, 14, 15, 139–40
feminism, 14, 38, 42–43, 44, 61, 62, 177–78
Fenians, 38, 63
Fennell, Dorothy, 26
Feuer, Lewis S., 38–39, 59
Fielden, Samuel, 163, 165, 169, 206
Fife, Alec, 190
Fink, Leon, 24, 221
First International (International Workingmen's Association), 38
Fischer, Adolph, 164, 169
Flower, Frank A., 82, 93, 124, 131, 132
Flynn, Elizabeth Gurley, 20, 33
Foner, Philip S., 22, 23, 24, 25, 147
Foster, William Z., 216
Fourier, Charles, 176
Frank, Isabell Campbell, 64
Frank, Lisa, 7
Freeman, Joshua, 26
Fried, Albert, 24
Frye, Eva, 40
Fukuyama, Francis, 65

Gary, Judge Joseph, 162, 163

Gentry, Gertrude, 36
Georgakas, Dan, 25
George, Henry, 55, 56, 134, 149, 151, 156, 171–75, 177, 180, 203, 204
Girard, Frank, 147
Glaberman, Martin, 26
Gompers, Samuel, 18–19, 24, 33, 147, 204, 215
Gould, Jay, 55, 95
Grange (Patrons of Husbandry), 14, 32, 139–40, 210
Grinnell, Julius, 162, 164
Grace, Mayor William Russell, 154
Gronlund, Laurence, 79
Guerin, Daniel, 159
gunboat diplomacy, 17
Gutman, Herbert, 23

Harrison, Mayor Carter, 165
Hartz, Louis, 8, 28
Hawkins, Lewis H., 175
Hayes, Rutherford B., 15
Haymarket affair and martyrs, 25, 38, 54, 56, 161–167, 168–69, 180–82, 183, 206–207, 210–11
Haywood, William ("Big Bill"), 17
Heine, Heinrich, 184
Hewitt, Abram, 134, 174
Hicks, Granville, 78
Hillquit, Morris, 23
Hinshaw, John, 22

Hinton, Colonel Richard J., 142, 171, 178–79, 180, 183
Hoagland, H. E., 22
Hooker, Isabella Beecher, 177
Howells, William Dean, 78
Howland, Edward and Marie, 175–76, 178
Huntington, Samuel, 65
Hyndman, Henry, 44, 58, 59

Ibsen, Henrik, 42
identities, 14
immigration, 11, 13, 19, 213, 214, 215, 219. *See also* racial and ethnic diversity
Indians (Native Americans), 12, 14, 29, 156
Industrial Workers of the World (IWW), 17, 19–20, 215, 216
International Labor Organization (ILO), 219
International Ladies Garment Workers Union, 19, 51, 213
International Working People's Organization, 168–70

James, C. L. R., 9, 28
James, Henry, 78
Kapp, Yvonne, 59, 60, 61
Kautsky, Karl, 61, 64
Kean, Edward J., 201
Kelly, Florence, 19, 33, 83, 190
Knights of Labor, 9, 15, 24, 38, 47,

54–55, 80, 116, 141–45, 146, 148, 149–50, 154, 155, 167, 174, 203, 204, 209, 210, 212, 220
Kuhn, Henry, 147

Labor Day, 19
labor history and working-class studies, 21–26, 29–31, 32–33, 34–35
labor laws, 19
Labor Movement in America, The (Ely), 134–35
Labor Notes, 27, 28
labor parties, 9, 10, 11, 16, 45, 47–48, 55–56, 66, 146, 149–51, 166, 173, 174, 175, 183, 209, 220
labor press, 9, 49, 70–72
Lafargue, Paul, 61
Lassalle, Ferdinand, 168, 180
Lassalleans, 33, 168
Latin Americans (in U.S.), 14
Laurie, Bruce, 22
Le Blanc, Paul, 22, 28
Lenin, Vladimir Ilyich, 51
Levine, Bruce, 26
Levine, Lawrence, 25
Levison, Andrew, 26
Lichtenstein, Nelson, 26
Liebknecht, Wilhelm, 47, 61, 64, 73, 161
Life in the Iron Mills (Davis), 78

Limerick, Patricia Nelson, 153
Lingg, Louis, 169, 206–207
Linnell, Alfred, 58
Lipow, Arthur, 204
Lipset, Seymour Martin, 8, 28
Lissagary, Prosper, 42
literature in the United States, 78, 204
Looking Backward (Bellamy), 204
Lorwin, Lewis, 24
Lovell, John W., 175, 177
Lumpkin, Katherine D., 190

MacCullough, Rev. William, 123
Mandel, Bernard, 23
Marx, Eleanor, 7, 8, 9, 11, 14, 16, 17, 19, 22, 27, 37–66, 209–12, 219
Marx, Jenny, 42, 58, 60
Marx, Karl, 7, 8, 9, 15–16, 18, 19, 20, 36, 38, 39, 41–42, 50, 53, 58, 61, 62, 82, 83, 147, 168, 169, 209
Marx, Laura, 45, 58, 64
Marxism, 7, 8, 14, 18–20, 22, 23, 24–25, 28, 36–39, 41, 50, 53, 65, 168–69, 209–10, 212
May Day, 56
McAllister, Carol, 27
McGuire, Peter J., 19, 33, 110, 187, 203, 210
McLemee, Scott, 27
Mehring, Franz, 51, 61

Meiksins, Peter, 26
Melville, Herman, 78
Meredith, George, 180, 184
Messer-Kruse, Timothy, 23
middle class ("bourgeois"—not working class), 75–76
Mittelman, E. B., 22
Moby Dick (Melville), 78
Montgomery, David, 23, 212
Moody, Kim, 7, 26, 66
Moore, Samuel, 60
Morais, Herbert M., 21, 35
Morgan, Thomas J., 183–84, 187
Morgan, William, 171, 183–84
Morris, William, 63–64, 204
Most, Johann, 54, 65, 160, 163, 169

nationalist movement (Bellamyites), 204–205
Natural Law in the Spirit World (Drummond), 205
Neebe, Oscar, 206
Nelson, Bruce, 25
News from Nowhere (Morris), 204
Nordhoff, Charles, 176
Noyes, John Humphrey, 176

Ohno, Taiichi, 218
Open Door Policy, 17
Owen, Albert K., 175
Owen, Robert, 175

Palmer, Bryan, 26
Paris Commune, 38, 42, 58
Parsons, Albert, 54, 65, 163, 165, 169
Paul, Daphne, 205
Peck, Charles F., 121, 127
Perlman, Selig, 22
Perry, Ben, 147
Pinkerton Detective Agency, 56
Plekhanov, George, 42, 159
Pombo, Ignacio, 175
populists, 14, 31–32, 210
Powderly, Terence V., 55, 144, 203
Progress and Poverty (George), 171
prostitution, 46–47, 122–23, 193–94
Proudhon, Pierre-Joseph, 168

Quint, Howard, 25

racial and ethnic diversity, 11, 13, 14, 30, 50–51, 59, 63, 146–47, 148–49, 168, 210, 211, 213, 215, 216, 219
racism, 12, 13–14, 30, 59, 210, 211, 212–13, 216
Racovitz, Helena von, 180
Randolph, A. Philip, 19, 33
Reconstruction era, 12, 15, 29, 212
Rediker, Marcus, 26
Religion, 123, 144, 187, 205

repression of labor, 13, 29, 56, 161–67, 206–207, 216; authoritarianism at workplace, 91–102, 110, 111, 123, 155, 156, 157–58, 197, 214; black list, 93–95, 102, 157; ironclad oath, 95–97
Republican Party, 10, 11, 15, 16, 19, 149, 150, 173, 174, 183, 212
Rideout, Walter, 78
Roediger, David, 24, 25, 170
Roman Catholic Church, 144
Rosebury, Aaron, 51, 60
Roosevelt, Theodore, 174
Rosemont, Franklin, 25, 170, 205
Rozenzweig, Roy, 25
Ruggles, W. B., 126
Russian Revolution, 65

Saint-Simon, Claude-Henri, 176
Samson, Leon, 8, 28
Saposs, David J., 22
Schevitch, Sergius, 171–80
Schanubelt, Rudolph, 164
Schoenfels, Kai, 23
Schor, Juliet, 24
Schwab, Michael, 165, 169, 206
scientific management, 211, 214, 215, 218
Second International (Socialist International), 42, 147
Seliger, Wilhelm, 164
Sexton, Patricia Cayo, 26

Shaiken, Harley, 26
Sinaloa community, 171, 175–77
Social Democratic Federation, 44, 60
socialism and socialists, 7, 8, 9, 12, 18–20, 24–25, 37–40, 41–42, 44, 45–47, 48, 50–54, 57–58, 61–64, 69–70, 73, 78–80, 143, 144, 145, 146–51, 159–61, 167, 168–70, 172, 174, 175–76, 182, 183–87, 204–205, 210, 211, 215, 216; lack of socialist movement in the United States, 8–9, 11–12, 52–53, 69–70, 79, 148; unconscious socialists in the United States, 8, 9, 17, 45, 54, 78–80, 144, 148, 150, 210
Socialist Labor Party, 40, 47, 54, 70, 80, 140, 146–49, 168, 186
Socialist League, 62–63
Socialist Party of America, 17, 215
Sombart, Werner, 65
Sorge, Friedrich, 23, 147, 168–69
Spargo, John, 190
Spencer, Charles, 26
Spies, August, 164, 165, 168–69
Stalinism, 8
Stephens, Uriah S., 141
Stowe, Harriet Beecher, 78, 177
Strasser, Adolph, 147
strikes, 47, 96, 132, 136, 144, 183, 199–201, 209, 211

Sullivan, John ("Broncho John"), 154–57, 158
Sumner, Helen L., 22

Taft, Philip, 22
Taylor, Frederick Winslow, 214
Terkel, Studs, 26
Tocqueville, Alexis de, 65
Toth, Csaba, 27, 205
trade unionism, 15, 17, 18–19, 20, 33–35, 42, 43, 45, 46, 47, 51, 55, 60, 62, 133, 134, 136–38, 155, 209–21; "pure and simple" unionism, 17, 22, 33, 133, 210. *See also* American Federation of Labor; Central Labor Unions; Congress of Industrial Organizations; Industrial Workers of the World; Knights of Labor; repression of labor; strikes; working class
Tragic Comedians (Meredith), 180
Trautman, Frederic, 169
Troester, Louis, 129

Uncle Tom's Cabin (Harriet Beecher Stowe), 78
Unitarians, 187
United Labor Party, 55, 136, 140, 149–51, 166, 173, 174
United Nations, 190, 218
United Shoe Workers, 215
utopian communities, 176–77

Vrooman, Walter and Harry, 171, 186–87

Walster, Otto, 184–85
Ward, Osborne, 184
Ware, Norman, 24
White, Richard, 153
Whitman, Walt, 78
Woman and Socialism (Bebel), 204–205
Woman Question, The (Aveling and Marx), 38, 59
woman suffrage, 171, 177–78
women, 14, 31, 38, 40, 42–43, 45–47, 59, 61–63, 115–23, 177–78, 190, 192–94, 204, 205, 213
Wood, Ellen Meiksins, 26
working class in the United States, 7–221; child labor, 19, 102, 115–16, 123–31, 190–91; compared with British workers, 81, 87–89, 99, 103, 107, 110–11, 113, 122, 123, 151, 195–96; compared with European workers, 11–12, 89; female labor, 115–23, 131, 190, 192–94; cowboys, 153–58; of workday, 89, 103, 106–107, 110, 128, 129–30, 194–95; intensity of labor, 84, 89, 103, 110–11, 114, 155, 156, 195; living conditions, 85–86, 88–

90, 103, 111–13, 118–21, 192; skilled/unskilled divergence, 210, 211–12, 213–14, 215, 216; unemployment, 85, 107–10, 196; wages, 84–90, 103–105, 116–18, 119, 123, 128–29, 155, 156, 192–93, 194, 216–17; working conditions, 84–90, 91–102, 116, 117, 118, 155, 156, 192, 197–99

World War I, 213, 215
Workingmen's Party of the United States, 146–47
Wright, Carroll D., 81, 109, 114, 130, 131, 199

Yates, Michael D., 24, 26
Young, Arthur, 171

Zinn, Howard, 29